Linking Assessment to Instruction in Multi-Tiered Models

A Teacher's Guide to Selecting Reading, Writing, and Mathematics Interventions

John J. Hoover

University of Colorado at Boulder

PEARSON

Boston   Columbus   Indianapolis   New York   San Francisco   Upper Saddle River
Amsterdam   Cape Town   Dubai   London   Madrid   Milan   Munich   Paris   Montreal   Toronto
Delhi   Mexico City   São Paulo   Sydney   Hong Kong   Seoul   Singapore   Taipei   Tokyo

Vice President and Editorial Director: Jeffery W. Johnston
Executive Editor: Ann Castel Davis
Vice President, Director of Marketing: Margaret Waples
Marketing Manager: Joanna Sabella
Senior Managing Editor: Pamela D. Bennett
Production Manager: Susan Hannahs
Photo Coordinator: Carol Sykes
Senior Art Director: Jayne Conte
Cover Designer: Suzanne Behnke
Cover Art: Ariel Skelley/Blend RF/Glow Images
Project Management: Rashmi Tickyani/Aptara®, Inc.
Composition: Aptara®, Inc.
Printer/Bindery: LSC Communications
Text Font: Minion Pro Regular

Photo Credits: © Atlaspix/Shutterstock, pp. 3, 162; © Palto/Shutterstock, pp. 19, 49, 65; © Reji/Shutterstock, p. 108; © Lorelyn Medina/Shutterstock, p. 138.

Credits and acknowledgments for material borrowed from other sources and reproduced, with permission, in this textbook appear on the appropriate page within the text.

Every effort has been made to provide accurate and current Internet information in this book. However, the Internet and information posted on it are constantly changing, so it is inevitable that some of the Internet addresses listed in this textbook will change.

Library of Congress Cataloging-in-Publication Data
Hoover, John J.
  Linking assessment to instruction in multi-tiered models : a teacher's guide to selecting reading, writing, and mathematics interventions / John J. Hoover, University of Colorado at Boulder.
    pages cm
  ISBN-13: 978-0-13-254267-8
  ISBN-10: 0-13-254267-6
  1. Remedial teaching.   2. Response to intervention (Learning disabled children)
3. Educational evaluation.   I. Title.
LB1029.R4H65 2013
371.9—dc23

2012016030

PEARSON

ISBN 10:   0-13-254267-6
ISBN 13: 978-0-13-254267-8

Preface

Context and Framework

Multi-tiered instruction is the foundation of the contemporary response-to-intervention (RTI) framework for educating all learners in today's classrooms. Although a multi-tiered instructional model has a significant impact at the district and school levels, the implementation at the classroom level is worthy of particular attention because it has direct effects on teaching and learning. In order to implement the model properly, teachers must have knowledge of its several components: (a) the structures that provide the foundation for the model, (b) the processes within which the delivery of instruction and assessment is completed, (c) interpretation of achievement data scores, and (d) selection and implementation of appropriate instructional interventions. Each of these components is discussed in detail in this text, and there is extensive coverage of structured evidence-based reading, writing, and mathematics interventions that are linked to achievement data. The multi-tiered model represents a comprehensive structural and educational paradigm shift, requiring collaboration among educators to best meet the needs of all learners.

Why Is This Text Needed?

In addition to drawing on the author's extensive research in and experiences with evidence-based practice in the content areas of reading, writing, and mathematics, this text used feedback from discussion and focus groups composed of current classroom teachers in both urban and rural school districts. The educators discussed the types of classroom achievement information they gathered, the achievement data scores their students earned, and how they collectively used the information to properly identify and implement needed instructional adjustments (e.g., classroom management, change from large- to small-group settings, more efficient use of student and/or teacher time, greater emphasis on cooperative than direct instruction, teaching intervention). Although a variety of topics emerged from the focus groups, the one consistent need expressed by educators who teach with multi-tiered models was increased guidance selecting appropriate interventions for a struggling learner.

Purpose of the Book

This experience and research suggested two important topics: processes to examine classroom and instructional elements associated with the achievement data scores, and suggested evidence-based interventions (EBIs) that lead to proper instructional adjustments, particularly in Tier 2 instruction. This text directly addresses these and related educator needs to assist teachers to make the most informed instructional adjustments grounded in achievement benchmark and progress monitoring data. Specifically, the purpose of this text is to provide practitioners links among universal screening, progress monitoring, and diagnostic scores with appropriate EBIs to meet the needs of learners in Tier 1, 2, or 3 instruction in the content areas of reading, writing, and mathematics.

For Whom Is This Text Written?

After achievement data indicate that a learner is struggling, practitioners are challenged to adjust instruction to meet learner needs. This text is written for current and future educators who rely on screening, progress monitoring, and diagnostic data to make instructional adjustments. It is suitable for use in professional development and university courses that emphasize multi-tiered instructional implementation and associated data collection. This implementation includes use in school district trainings, graduate and undergraduate curricular methods, assessment classes, and other similar workshop trainings.

Overview

Linking Assessment to Instruction in Multi-Tiered Models: A Teacher's Guide to Selecting Reading, Writing, and Mathematics Interventions presents the most up-to-date evidence-based practice in each of the three content areas of reading, writing, and mathematics. The text contains seven chapters divided into two parts:

> *Part I: Framework, Process, and Collaboration in Multi-Tiered Instructional Models*
>
> Chapter 1: Structure of Multi-Tiered Instructional Models
> Chapter 2: Process of Multi-Tiered Instructional Models
> Chapter 3: Collaboration to Implement Instructional Adjustments
>
> *Part II: Reading, Writing, and Mathematics Interventions*
>
> Chapter 4: Evidence-Based Reading Practices
> Chapter 5: Evidence-Based Writing Practices

Chapter 6: Evidence-Based Mathematics Practices

Chapter 7: Concluding Remarks: Meeting the Classroom Challenges of Multi-Tiered Instruction

Part I covers the multi-tiered instructional model found within an RTI framework, screening and progress monitoring, methods to analyze and improve differentiated classroom instructional and behavioral management, and the process for making team instructional decisions through collaboration.

Part II presents key evidence-based practices for use in multi-tiered models to meet the learning needs of students in the content areas of reading, writing, and mathematics. Specifically, it provides numerous structured EBIs that include sufficient information for practitioners to best select and use the interventions, using achievement and other supporting student data. Readers will learn the steps and expected outcomes for each intervention to guide its implementation with students in the classroom. Specific linkages to and applications of achievement data are provided to guide selection of appropriate interventions to meet multi-tiered instructional needs.

Key Features

To facilitate the practical application of the contents of this text, the chapters include overviews, key terms, and numerous figures, tables, charts, and guides for use in the teaching and learning environment. These features assist practitioners to use universal screening, progress monitoring, and diagnostic data to select appropriate teaching interventions and to make effective instructional adjustments in collaborative ways. Collectively, *Linking Assessment to Instruction in Multi-Tiered Models: A Teacher's Guide to Selecting Reading, Writing, and Mathematics Interventions* provides nearly 100 strategies, interventions, and curricula in the content areas of reading, writing, and mathematics, as illustrated:

Interventions and Strategy Types	
Number	**Curricula, Strategies, and Interventions**
16	Proven Classroom and Instructional Management Techniques
23	Research-Based Reading, Writing, and Mathematics Curricula to Meet Significant Needs
27	Evidence-Based Reading, Writing, and Mathematics Structured Interventions
30	Proven Student Study Skills and Strategies

The proper selection and application of these 96 instructional items, strategically implemented within the structure and process of a multi-tiered model, empowers all learners and their teachers to effectively meet reading, writing, and mathematics needs through core Tier 1 instruction, supplemental Tier 2 supports, and intensive Tier 3 interventions in timely and preventative ways.

Acknowledgments

Thank you to my reviewers for their helpful comments and suggestions: Bert Chiang, University of Wisconsin; Suzanne Graney, Rochester Institute of Technology; and Ashli Tyre, Seattle University. In addition, a special thanks is extended to the following practitioners for their review of the interventions and for their insightful classroom-based suggestions: Megan Moran, Shannon White, Audrey Frey, Angie Van Decar, Robin Hoover, and Cassie Harrelson.

About the Author

Dr. John J. Hoover is Associate Research Professor in the Graduate School of Education at the University of Colorado at Boulder specializing in multicultural special education instruction and assessment. He is a former special education teacher and supervisor instructing students with learning, intellectual and emotional disabilities in grades K-12. He also has numerous years of administrative and supervisory experiences in research and teacher training in multicultural and special education over that past 30 years. His work in the field of education is well-documented as he has over 65 publications in multicultural, special and general education. Since 2008, Dr. Hoover has authored or co-authored 4 journal articles, 4 books, and 3 textbook chapters in addition to delivering numerous workshop and conference sessions on multi-tiered response to intervention addressing the interrelated topics of evidence-based interventions, RTI and special education, progress monitoring data collection, and school RTI team decision-making. Recent publications include: *Early Reading Assessment Diagnostic Test* (2012, Pro-Ed) *Response to Intervention: Curricular Implications and Interventions* (2011, Pearson); *RTI Assessment Essentials for Struggling Learners* (2009, Corwin Press); and *Differentiating Learning Differences from Disabilities: Meeting Diverse Needs Through Multi-Tiered Response to Intervention* (2009, Pearson).

John J. Hoover

Contents

Figures, Tables, and Forms

PART I

Framework, Process, and Collaboration in Multi-Tiered Instructional Models

CHAPTER 1

Structure of Multi-Tiered Instructional Models

▶ ## Chapter Overview

THE CORNERSTONE OF TODAY'S instructional framework is the implementation of effective multi-tiered assessment and instruction that are validated through research to meet the needs of all learners. Chapter 1 provides an overview of the structure of multi-tiered instruction within a response-to-intervention (RTI) framework describing the key components that are necessary to successfully teach all learners. Multi-tiered models require an interaction between assessment and instruction that challenges educators to manage both assessment processes and instructional adjustments simultaneously in any teaching and learning setting.

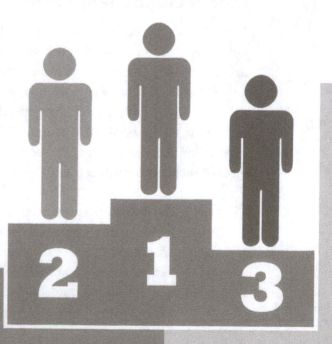

▶ Key Terms

- ▶ Diagnostic assessment
- ▶ Differentiated instruction
- ▶ Evidence-based interventions
- ▶ Evidence-based practice
- ▶ Multi-tiered instruction
- ▶ Progress monitoring
- ▶ Research-based curriculum
- ▶ Universal screening

Overview of Multi-Tiered Instructional Models

Although many educators are generally familiar with **multi-tiered instruction**, a review of its key components provides the reader with a sufficient grounding to best understand the central focus of this text (i.e., **evidence-based assessment** leading to evidence-based instructional adjustments). The purpose of these discussions is to address key aspects that are necessary to implement a multi-tiered model, rather than to provide detailed coverage of this model. The reader is referred to the sources cited in this section for more in-depth coverage of multi-tiered instructional models. Five key components comprise the structure of many multi-tiered models found in today's elementary and secondary classrooms: (a) tiered instruction; (b) high-quality instruction; (c) evidence-based practice; (d) screening, monitoring, and diagnostic assessment; and (e) instructional fidelity.

Model Component 1: Tiered Instruction

Multi-tiered instruction is delivered within a schoolwide framework that provides layers or tiers of instruction to students. Although a variety of tiers may exist, most models include three tiers of instruction (Fuchs & Fuchs, 2006; Mellard & Johnson, 2008; Vaughn, 2003) as illustrated in Figure 1.1.

As shown, each tier reflects a specific type of instruction designed collectively to meet the needs of all learners. The duration and intensity of necessary instruction increases with each tier as learners progress. Here is a brief overview of each tier of instruction.

TIER 1 ■ The initial instructional tier is the core instruction that is delivered to all students in the classroom. Expectations are that Tier 1 instruction facilitates success for at least 80% of the students, measured by progress toward grade-level benchmarks (Yell, 2004). Within a multi-tiered model, if fewer than 80% of learners do not make adequate progress, the first course of action is to

FIGURE 1.1   Multi-Tiered Model Structure

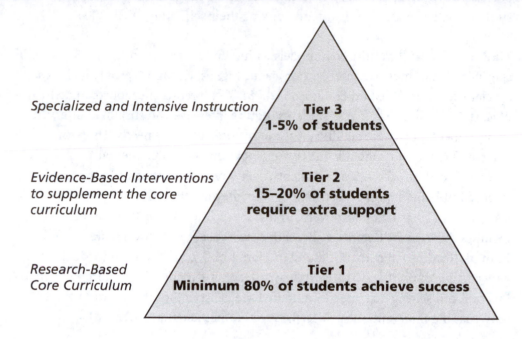

adjust or differentiate the Tier 1 instruction to meet the instructional and behavioral needs of most learners. Several key educational components are found within comprehensive Tier 1 instruction that are necessary to meet the needs of all learners: (a) research-based curriculum (RBC), (b) evidence-based interventions (EBIs), (c) differentiated instruction (DI), and (d) sufficient opportunities to learn (deemed sufficient if 80% of students achieve at benchmark). These four educational components are essential to providing high-quality evidence-based practice, which is the foundation of a multi-tiered instructional model. Each of these four educational components is discussed in greater detail in a subsequent section of this chapter.

TIER 2 ■ Learners who struggle, are at risk to struggle, or are unsuccessful at learning even with properly implemented Tier 1 instruction receive supplemental supports referred to as Tier 2 instruction (Bender & Shores, 2007; Fuchs & Fuchs, 2006). Tier 2 instruction is designed to supplement Tier 1 instruction and not replace it; all students who receive Tier 2 supports also receive all Tier 1 instruction. Therefore, it is important to avoid providing students with Tier 2 supports at a time when other students are receiving new Tier 1 instruction. Tiers 1 and 2 instruction complement and support each other and may be provided as push-in or pull-out arrangements implemented by an interventionist, general educator, special educator, or other support professional. Effective Tier 2 instruction includes providing supplemental support to small groups of learners with similar needs. However, the greater the connection between Tiers

1 and 2 instruction provided by the general class teacher, the greater the continuity across teaching and learning, leading to more effective instructional supports (Hoover & Love, 2011). Estimates are that a range of 15%–20% of students will require Tier 2 supports during their schooling (Yell, 2004).

TIER 3 ■ In most multi-tiered models within an RTI framework, Tier 3 (i.e., specialized and intensive intervention) is the highest tier and typically includes special education (Mellard & Johnson, 2008). Tier 3 represents approximately 5% of learners (Yell, 2004). These students require intensive and sustained interventions to meet their more significant academic or behavioral needs. Therefore, whereas Tiers 1 and 2 include the core curriculum and supplemental supports to meet the needs of 90%–95% of students, Tier 3 represents the need for more intense implementation of instruction, going beyond that which is possible in Tiers 1 and 2 instruction (Hoover, 2011a). Tier 3 intensive instruction often includes the use of different or alternative curricula (e.g., Wilson Reading, Edmark Reading) that are not found in Tiers 1 or 2, provided to individuals or very small groups of up to three students. Tier 3 instruction is often implemented in a pull-out setting delivered by a trained specialist in the content area of need (e.g., reading interventionist, special educator, mathematics specialist).

Model Component 2: High-Quality Instruction

For the past few decades, struggling learners' needs were formally met only after a significant amount of time elapsed (up to 2 years). This practice was grounded in the prereferral intervention model that led to thousands of students being placed in special education over the past 30 years; many of them would have had their needs met if interventions were provided in a more timely, preventative manner. Therefore, a cornerstone of multi-tiered models is the initial emphasis on implementing high-quality instruction rather than seeking "intrinsic" disorders within the struggling student (Hoover, 2010). The emphasis on high-quality instruction challenges all educators to provide evidence-based education implemented in the manner in which it was researched and validated. A multi-tiered instructional model with an RTI framework varies from previous prereferral models in that the initial course of action is to ensure that the struggling student has been provided high-quality Tier 1 instruction. If high-quality instruction was not provided, adjustments to the Tier 1 core instruction must be made prior to considering whether the learner has intrinsic disorders. This approach represents a significant shift away from the previous prereferral intervention model (i.e., wait to fail) to the contemporary multi-tiered model (i.e., engage in early intervention and prevention). Now educators must confirm that high-quality instruction exists before they consider more intensive instruction (i.e., Tiers 2 or 3) or special education. Table 1.1, developed from information found in Hoover (2011b), compares prereferral and multi-tiered instructional model practices.

TABLE 1.1 Comparing Prereferral and Multi-Tiered Instructional Practices

Prereferral Practices	Multi-Tiered Practices
Prereferral Model provides struggling learners with two types of instruction (Prereferral Interventions and Special Education)	*Multi-Tiered Model* includes three instructional types: Core, Supplemental, Intensive
Academic/behavioral school-wide screening not typically completed	Screening occurs for all learners in academics and behavior, often three times per year
Research-based curriculum may not always be used in general class core instruction	Core instruction in general classroom must be validated through research
Evidence-based interventions may or may not be used in the classroom	All interventions must be validated as evidence-based
Primary method for identifying a learning disability is determination of a discrepancy between intellectual capacity and actual achievement	Achievement-intellectual discrepancy is de-emphasized; greater emphasis is placed on the actual versus expected achievement discrepancy to determine a learning disability
Norm-referenced measures are used extensively to assess struggling learners	Curriculum-based measures are the preferred method of choice to assess progress of struggling learners
Assessment decision making focuses on "intrinsic" disorders within the learner	Assessment decision making focuses on "quality of instruction" for the learner
Progress of struggling learner is infrequently monitored in the general classroom core instruction	Progress is regularly monitored after a student begins to struggle in school
At-risk/struggling learners are initially identified after having exhibited problems for an extended period of time.	All learners are initially screened to identify those who show signs of struggling early in schooling
Learners making inadequate progress with the general class core curriculum must receive a comprehensive evaluation prior to being provided extended curricular supports	Targeted supports are provided to struggling learners in the general class core instruction prior to giving them a special education comprehensive evaluation
Primary model used with struggling learners is a "wait to fail" model	Primary model used with struggling learners is a preventative and early intervening model

Model Component 3: Evidence-Based Practice

Multi-tiered instruction is grounded in the implementation of **evidence-based practice** (i.e., practice that is based on validated curricula and interventions shown by research to be effective). This foundation is necessary to provide quality multi-tiered instruction (Haager, Klingner, & Vaughn, 2007; Hoover, 2011b; Moran & Malott, 2004). Evidence-based practice is illustrated in Figure 1.2 and includes, at minimum, three key elements found in the instructional environment reflecting validation research for (a) a research-based curriculum, (b) evidence-based interventions, and (c) differentiated instruction.

Ultimately, the goal of any multi-tiered model is to reduce unnecessary referrals, prevent problems from becoming more severe by engaging in early identification and prevention, and provide sufficient opportunities for students

FIGURE 1.2 Three Components of Evidence-Based Practice

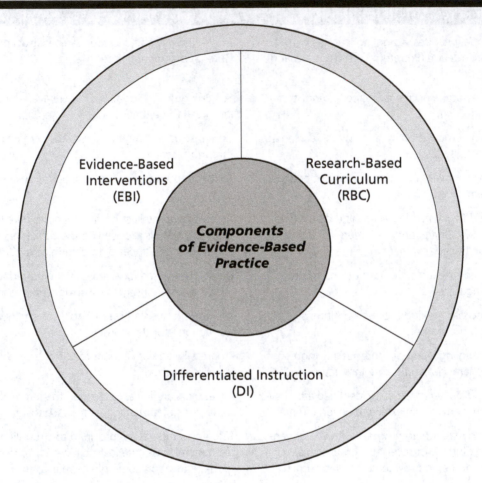

to learn so that 80% or more of the students succeed. All three of these instructional elements are necessary to provide comprehensive evidence-based practice, as they are implemented in integrated ways to deliver multi-tiered instruction (Hoover, 2011a).

RESEARCH-BASED CURRICULUM ■ A **research-based curriculum** (RBC) includes a comprehensive content or social-emotional educational program that provides educators with most or all necessary materials, teaching instructions, supplemental or guided activities, and related elements typically found within a complete program. Examples of RBCs include comprehensive programs such as Edmark Reading, Mathematics Investigations, Success for All, Saxon Math, Hermann Reading, Ladders to Literacy, Literacy by Design, and Wilson Reading System. An RBC is used to deliver instruction in any instructional tier that provides learners a comprehensive program in specific content areas. Subsequent chapters provide additional discussion of RBCs in the content areas addressed in this text (i.e., reading, writing, mathematics).

EVIDENCE-BASED INTERVENTIONS ■ Whereas an RBC includes a comprehensive program, **Evidence-based interventions** (EBIs) include specific methods that are used to support Tier 1 core instruction, supplement Tier 1 instruction through Tier 2 supports, or provide primary strategies to meet the more intensive needs of students who exhibit more significant problems (i.e., students who are Tier 3). EBIs are structured methods that are validated through research to be effective in the teaching and learning environment, containing prescribed procedures detailing teacher and learner expectations. Examples of EBIs include reciprocal teaching, classwide peer tutoring, and direct instruction. It is essential, when selecting and implementing an EBI, to ensure that the method is used in the way in which it was designed and validated, adhering to established procedures. EBIs found in the content areas discussed in this text are presented in subsequent chapters.

DIFFERENTIATED INSTRUCTION ■ Sufficient opportunities to learn best occur in classrooms that are shaped by differentiated instructional and classroom management (Hoover, 2011b; Tomlinson, 2001). Although RBC and EBIs provide the necessary grounding for multi-tiered instruction, use of commonly accepted differentiated instruction complements any classroom environmental structure. **Differentiated instruction** (DI) represents the various teacher and student strategies that are easy to implement and that fit within any type of curricula to provide a balanced and structured classroom. These types of strategies include planned ignoring, proximity control, repetition of directions, appropriate use of student groupings, consistent rewards and consequences, and other similar instructional and classroom methods that accommodate the various learning preferences, needs, expectations, and experiential backgrounds typically found in today's classrooms. DI should be used in each tier of instruction and is particularly important in determining the effectiveness of Tier 1 instruction for all students, especially those who are struggling. Overall, DI is essential to implementing evidence-based practice to provide sufficient opportunities to learn for all students.

Distinguishing among RBC, EBI, and DI is critical, as it helps practitioners to more easily interpret student achievement data scores and results, leading to more appropriate instructional adjustments. "This breakdown allows teachers to view classroom instructional needs within a multi-tiered model from both an overall and specific instructional perspective" (Hoover & Love, 2011, p. 41). That is, in some instances the addition of more targeted differentiated strategies within Tier 1 instruction may be all that is needed to assist a struggling learner, reducing the need for more resource-intensive Tier 2 supports. Identifying the most appropriate type of evidence-based practice is key to accurately adjusting instruction that is based on achievement data that reflect the three content areas emphasized in this text (i.e., reading, writing, mathematics). Distinguishing among RBC, EBI, and DI is examined in greater detail in Chapter 2, in which the process of the multi-tiered instructional model is described.

Model Component 4: Screening, Monitoring, and Performing Diagnostic Assessment

Along with the need to deliver the three components of evidence-based practice, a multi-tiered model contains key assessment components to provide high-quality instruction to all learners. These components include the three primary assessment types discussed here.

UNIVERSAL SCREENING ■ **Universal screening** includes early efforts to identify learners who struggle in school (usually conducted three times per year). The primary purpose of universal screening is to identify learners who are at risk or those who may be showing signs of struggling in learning, in order to provide early and preventative supports. Universal screening also assists in identifying classrooms and teachers who may require additional supports to best implement Tier 1 core instruction (National Association of State Directors of Special Education, 2005).

PROGRESS MONITORING ■ **Progress monitoring** is a research-based assessment method that is used to monitor learner progress toward benchmarks on a more frequent basis (e.g., monthly, biweekly). Progress monitoring is fundamental to documenting how a student progresses and the extent to which implementation of Tiers 1, 2, or 3 instruction is effective in meeting learner needs.

DIAGNOSTIC ASSESSMENT ■ **Diagnostic assessment** is an individualized form of assessment that is used to pinpoint individual learner needs. Diagnostic assessment is best used in conjunction with universal screening and progress monitoring. It assists school teams to develop appropriate instructional adjustments for struggling learners, including the development of individual education plans (IEPs).

These three assessments vary significantly from assessments that were used before the widespread implementation of multi-tiered models. Knowledge of several key assessment competencies is helpful to best understand their application within multi-tiered models, as discussed by Hoover (2009a) and summarized in Table 1.2.

The process of use of each of the three assessment types is described further in Chapter 2.

Model Component 5: Instructional Fidelity

One of the more controversial issues surrounding the misplacement of learners into special education is the persistent emphasis on determining what might be

TABLE 1.2 Screening, Monitoring, and Performing Diagnostic Assessment in Multi-Tiered Instruction

Competency	Description
Know Assessment Purposes	Educators must know the purposes of universal screening, progress monitoring, and diagnostic assessments. They should know *why* each type of assessment exists, when each is best used, and for which purposes the assessment scores will be applied.
Instruction-Assessment Connection	Curriculum implementation and assessment are directly connected, as assessment results are used to initially determine that the students were taught properly. In addition, instruction-assessment connections directly reflect student progress toward benchmarks rather than emphasis on what might be "wrong" with the learner.
Know Assessment Procedures	Knowledge about *how* to properly implement screening, monitoring, and diagnostic assessments is essential to achieve assessment competence. Whether or not they are involved directly in the implementation of assessment, all educators should be familiar with procedures followed to gather screening, monitoring, and diagnostic data.
Charting Results	This competency reflects abilities to accurately chart or graph assessment data for individual, small, and large groups of students. Commercial screening and monitoring measures and procedures exist, such as AIMSweb, which is featured in Chapter 2; however, not all districts choose these services, and charting becomes a task that is conducted at the school or district level. Proficiency with the charting of assessment data is essential to successfully implementing an overall multi-tiered intervention model.
Interpreting Results	After assessments have been properly implemented and data have been charted, educators must accurately interpret those results. Specifically, they must interpret assessment scores relative to (a) proficiency level (i.e., the cut-off score below which a student is considered to be at risk or struggling) and (b) rate of progress toward achieving benchmarks for age and/or grade-level peers. Multi-tiered assessment data are in turn used to make instructional adjustment decisions.
Decision-Making Rules	Guidelines used by school teams to make instructional decisions on the basis of assessment data or results must be established and adhered to in the decision-making process. Educators should be familiar with the "decision rules" their school teams use to best interpret screening, monitoring, or diagnostic results.

"wrong" with the student, rather than on whether quality instruction has been provided (Fuchs & Fuchs, 2006). To address this issue, one of the key differences between the previous prereferral and the contemporary multi-tiered instructional model (see Table 1.1) is the need to confirm that quality instruction has been provided prior to initiating special education placement procedures. As discussed, a multi-tiered model requires the implementation of RBCs, EBIs, and DI to ensure quality of instruction. However, a key component in the process of interpreting universal screening, progress monitoring, and diagnostic results is not only to confirm that RBC, EBIs, and DI have been implemented but also to confirm that each has been properly implemented. In other words, checking instruction or implementation fidelity can rule out poor or inappropriate instruction as a primary reason for the lack of progress in a struggling learner. Should it be determined that RBC, EBIs, and/or DI do not exist or are not being implemented properly (i.e., low fidelity), ensuring that instructional fidelity occurs is the first choice for instructional adjustments. Any significant deviations from the research-validated procedures found within RBC, EBIs, or DI negatively affects implementation integrity, often resulting in lack of progress. "Therefore, educators must make certain that all instruction and associated assessments are properly implemented and that evidence exists to confirm their proper implementation (e.g., direct observations; interviews; video-taped lessons)" (Hoover, 2011a, p. 85). Forms 1.1 (*Fidelity of Implementation of Research-Based Curriculum*) and 1.2 (*Fidelity of Implementation of Evidence-Based Interventions*) at the end of this chapter provide guides to document the existence of fidelity of implementation of RBC and EBIs within multi-tiered instruction.

Form 1.3 (*Multi-Tiered Structure Evaluation Guide*), developed from information found in Hoover (2011b; 2009a,b) provides classroom teachers and other educators the opportunity to document that the proper structure is in place by including the five key multi-tiered components. This form also is found at the end of the chapter. As shown, each of the five key components is represented for educators to indicate that the multi-tiered instructional structure in their schools and classrooms is properly maintained. Educators should complete the guide periodically to ensure that the structure of the model includes all five components necessary to maintain a solid foundation for success in the classroom.

CONCLUSION

The multi-tiered instructional model within an RTI framework includes several key components for proper implementation in schools and classrooms. Multi-tiered instruction is characterized by tiered instruction, high-quality instruction, evidence-based practice, assessment, and instructional fidelity. Each of these components is essential for success in meeting the academic instructional needs of all learners, especially those who may struggle in reading, writing, and mathematics.

Title of RBC: _____

Content/Topic Area Addressed: _____

Primary Method(s) for Completion (Check each that applies):

_____ Direct Observation by Colleague   _____ Self-Reporting   _____ Interview

Instructions: Record evidence that corroborates the extent of implementation of the RBC. Provide comments as appropriate.

1 = Little/None   2 = Some but Limited   3 = Adequate   4 = Extensive

The Extent the Identified RBC is . . .

_____ Clearly understood by the teacher
Comments:

_____ Consistently implemented in the classroom
Comments:

_____ Differentiated appropriately to meet a variety of learning needs
Comments:

_____ Applied in teaching and learning for the specific purpose(s) it was designed
Comments:

_____ Implemented adhering to all recommended and prescribed steps and procedures
Comments:

_____ Supplemented for struggling learners to meet targeted needs
Comments:

_____ Implemented in a manner that facilitates effective teacher–student interactions
Comments:

_____ Integrated into overall classroom structure by facilitating effective proximity between teacher and students
Comments:

Summary of Fidelity of Implementation of RBC:

FORM 1.2 Fidelity of Implementation of Evidence-Based Interventions

Title of EBI: _____

Content/Topic Area Addressed: _____

Primary Method(s) for Completion (Check each that applies):

_____ Direct Observation by Colleague   _____ Self-Reporting   _____ Interview

Instructions: Record evidence that corroborates the extent of implementation of the EBI. Provide comments as appropriate.

| 1 = Little/None | 2 = Some but Limited | 3 = Adequate | 4 = Extensive |

The Extent the Identified EBI is . . .

___ Clearly understood by the teacher
Comments:

___ Consistently implemented in the classroom
Comments:

___ Differentiated appropriately to meet a variety of learning needs
Comments:

___ Applied in teaching and learning for the specific purpose(s) it was designed
Comments:

___ Implemented adhering to all recommended and prescribed steps and procedures
Comments:

___ Supplemented for struggling learners to meet targeted needs
Comments:

___ Implemented in a manner that facilitates effective teacher–student interactions
Comments:

___ Integrated into overall classroom structure by facilitating effective proximity between teacher and students
Comments:

Summary of Fidelity of Implementation of EBI:

School: _____   Date Completed: _____

Grade Level: ___ Primary (K–3)
(check all   ___ Intermediate (4–5)
that apply)   ___ Middle (6–8)
                    ___ Secondary 9–12)

School Decision-Making Team Members (List Primary Team Members):

_____   _____
_____   _____
_____   _____

Instructions: Check the multi-tiered components currently in place in your school. (Check all that apply and provide any relevant comments for each item.)

I. Multi-Tiered Instructional Levels

___ Tier 1 core instruction is appropriate for students in all grades (check areas):
         ___ Reading
         ___ Writing
         ___ Mathematics

Comments:

___ Appropriate practices and procedures for providing Tier 2 Supplemental Supports are established for all grades (check areas):
         ___ Reading
         ___ Writing
         ___ Mathematics

Comments:

___ Appropriate practices and procedures for providing Tier 3 Intensive Interventions are established for all grades (check areas):
         ___ Reading
         ___ Writing
         ___ Mathematics

Comments:

___ School-based multi-tiered decision-making team has been established

Comments:

(continued)

II. High-Quality Instruction

___ Research-Based Curriculum (RBC) is in place for all grades (check areas):
> ___ Reading
> ___ Writing
> ___ Mathematics

Comments:

___ Approved RBCs have been identified and used for Tier 3 instruction for all grades (check areas):
> ___ Reading
> ___ Writing
> ___ Mathe*matics*

Comments:

___ Approved Evidence-Based Interventions (EBIs) have been identified and used for Tier 2 instruction for all grades (check areas):
> ___ Reading
> ___ Writing
> ___ Mathematics

___ Approved EBIs have been identified and used for Tier 3 instruction for all grades (check areas):
> ___ Reading
> ___ Writing
> ___ Mathematics

Comments:

III. Evidence-Based Practice

___ Tier 1 RBC is in place for all grades (check areas):
> ___ Reading
> ___ Writing
> ___ Mathematics

Comments:

___ Differentiated instruction is implemented in Tier 1 instruction (check areas):
> ___ Reading
> ___ Writing
> ___ Mathematics

Comments:

___ Tier 2 supplemental instruction includes use of EBIs (check areas):
       ___ Reading
       ___ Writing
       ___ Mathematics

Comments:

___ Tier 3 intensive instruction includes use of RBCs (check areas):
       ___ Reading
       ___ Writing
       ___ Mathematics

Comments:

___ Tier 3 intensive instruction includes use of EBIs (check areas):
       ___ Reading
       ___ Writing
       ___ Mathematics

Comments:

VI. Screening, Monitoring, and Performing Diagnostic Assessment

___ Universal Screening exists for all students (check areas):
       ___ Reading
       ___ Writing
       ___ Mathematics

Comments:

___ *Curriculum-based progress-monitoring procedures exist in all classrooms (check areas):*
       ___ *Reading*
       ___ *Writing*
       ___ *Mathematics*

Comments:

___ Diagnostic assessment is implemented when necessary to pinpoint individual needs in all grade levels (check areas):
       ___ Reading
       ___ Writing
       ___ Mathematics

Comments:

(continued)

V. Instructional Fidelity

___ Fidelity of implementation contains process for corroborating effective instruction using

        ___ Tier 1 RBC

        ___ Tier 2 supplemental supports

        ___ Tier 3 intensive interventions

Comments:

___ Fidelity of implementation contains process for corroborating effective assessment:

        ___ Universal Screening

        ___ Progress Monitoring

        ___ Diagnostic

Comments:

___ School-wide data-driven decision-making procedures are clearly articulated

Comments:

___ *Procedures for referring a learner for special education are established*

Comments:

___ Procedures for determining special education eligibility for learning disabilities are established

Comments:

CHAPTER 2

Process of Multi-Tiered Instructional Models

▶ ## Chapter Overview

WITHIN THE STRUCTURE OF multi-tiered models presented in the previous chapter are certain processes that should be implemented in an organized manner to best meet the needs of all students. Chapter 2 describes the process for successfully implementing a multi-tiered instructional model. Similar to previous models or frameworks seen in our educational system, multi-tiered instruction requires educators to follow specific procedures for delivering and evaluating classroom instruction. Adherence to the process described in this chapter empowers educators to effectively provide instruction, screen student learning, and monitor progress, while using achievement data to make appropriate instructional adjustments.

Key Terms

- AIMSweb
- Diagnostic assessment
- Gap analysis
- Instructional adjustments
- Multi-tiered process
- Proficiency cut score
- Progress monitoring
- Rate of progress
- Universal screening

INTRODUCTION

The *structures* presented in the previous chapter provide educators with the foundational components that are necessary for successful implementation of a multi-tiered model within the framework of RTI. However, the defined structures in the model exist primarily for the purpose of delivering and evaluating instruction with fidelity, effectiveness, and monitored results. Embedded within the structures for delivering high-quality instruction is the process for examining and interpreting student progress results. This process includes (a) instructional delivery; (b) the process of universal screening, progress monitoring, and diagnostic assessment; (c) interpretation of achievement data; and (d) a framework for making instructional adjustments. These topics comprise the *process* of multi-tiered models, and are presented in detail in this chapter to illustrate the proper sequence in the selection and use of instructional interventions and in implementing the continuum of assessment. Various programs exist for screening and monitoring student progress within RTI models. We will focus on one of the more popular programs, AIMSweb, as an illustration of an effective way to examine learner academic achievement while reflecting the assessment and instruction process.

Multi-Tiered Instructional Delivery Process

A multi-tiered model requires the systematic and structured delivery of curriculum that increases in intensity and duration as the learner progresses. The following discussion covers each of the steps in instructional delivery. It is essential that these are completed in the proper sequence to ensure effective implementation.

Step 1: Implement an RBC, including appropriated differentiations, in the general education classroom for all learners (Tier 1 instruction).

Step 2: Implement, in the general education classroom, more targeted DI for those students who experience learning problems or who are at risk for learning problems (Tier 1 instruction).

Step 3: Implement in small-group settings, either as push-in or pull-out, with selected EBIs to provide additional and supplemental support for students who have not progressed adequately in response to instruction as described in steps 1 and 2 (Tier 2 instruction).

Step 4: Consider the use of an alternative curriculum that differs from that which is taught in steps 1, 2, and 3 (Tier 3 instruction).

Therefore, the accepted instructional process within a multi-tiered model is to implement an RBC, targeted differentiations, and selected EBIs, followed by use of alternate curricula. Examples of RBCs in reading, writing, and mathematics are provided in Chapters 4, 5, and 6 respectively. DI employs the use of a variety of teaching and behavior management techniques and study strategies, such as those presented in Tables 2.1 and 2.2. Structured EBIs in reading, writing, and mathematics are also provided in Chapters 4, 5, and 6 respectively, as are examples of alternate or different curricula.

NOTE: Use of an RBC, differentiated teaching and behavior management techniques, study strategies, and the structured EBIs occurs PRIOR to use of alternate or different curricula within a multi-tiered instructional model.

The following example summarizes the proper implementation of the instructional process.

A second-grade student is taught reading in the general second-grade classroom through use of an RBC (e.g., Houghton-Mifflin Reading Program). This student begins to experience difficulties and is struggling in reading class. The teacher then selects and implements two DI teaching techniques (i.e., contingency contracting, self-monitoring) to help the student in reading. Both of these instructional strategies fall within Tier 1 instruction. After the student continues to show lack of progress with the research-based reading curriculum and the targeted instructional differentiations as demonstrated by poor achievement data scores, the teacher selects and implements a structured reading intervention (e.g., reciprocal teaching) that is delivered for several weeks in a small-group setting. The implementation of the structured reading intervention in a small-group setting falls within Tier 2 instruction. If, after two rounds of use of the structured reading intervention, the learner continues to make inadequate progress, the teacher may consider an alternate curriculum (e.g., Wilson Reading, Orton-Gillingham). NOTE: The selection and use of the alternate curriculum occurs only after the implementation of one or more structured EBIs. Too often, the decision is made to move from the RBC and differentiated teaching and behavior management techniques to the alternate curriculum, skipping the critical step of using structured EBIs.

TABLE 2.1 Teaching and Behavior Management Techniques in Multi-Tiered Curriculum Implementation

Technique	Description	Desired Outcomes	RTI Considerations
Learning Center	Designated area where instructional materials are available for use by individuals or small groups of students	Students reinforce learning at own pace	Center may contain activities that reinforce areas of needed support
Alternative Method for Response	Mode of response is adapted for learners	Students respond to learning in a manner consistent with their needs	Differentiated response modes supports varying styles and these should be respected by teachers
Shortened Assignments	Assignments are broken into shorter, more manageable tasks	Difficult or complex tasks are more easily completed by students	Students with shorter attention spans or those who require more time to complete tasks in any tier of instruction may initially respond better to shorter assignments
Role Playing	Students assume roles and act out their perceptions of the roles	Students acquire a greater understanding of acceptable behaviors in different situations	Role play is one technique to assist learners to address social-emotional objectives in any tier of instruction
Providing Choices	Students have the opportunity to select tasks or assignments of their choice or to choose the order in which they complete tasks	Assists students to manage time and organize their completion of assignments; Students reduce anxiety with assignment completion	Learners manage time and organize themselves on the basis of their preferred instructional styles and prior experiences with curricular expectations
Contingency Contracting	Teacher and student prepare a formal agreement concerning academics or behaviors	Improves motivation; Supports preferred ways of learning; Students assume greater ownership in learning	Learning goals may be incorporated into contracts; A variety of academic or behavioral needs may be accommodated through contracts within RTI
Modify Presentation of Abstract Concepts	Scaffolding; Use of concrete procedures to assist learners with abstract concepts	Abstract concepts are made more comprehensible to learners with differing linguistic or cognitive abilities	Technique builds on student's prior experiences to increase success with new, challenging material
Prompting	Provide cues and supports to facilitate learning and response	Support learning to encourage and maintain interest and success	Alerts students to upcoming transitions or the need to self-manage time or behavior within RTI classroom or instructional management
Simplify Reading Levels	Reduce and minimize the complexities of language and vocabulary in printed material	Provide learners with language and vocabulary commensurate with their English language development	Learners must access the curriculum at points commensurate with abilities and this technique facilitates appropriate access

TABLE 2.1 (Continued)

Technique	Description	Desired Outcomes	RTI Considerations
Signal Interference	Nonverbal cues or signals to manage behavior or support student actions	Prevent minor behaviors from becoming more significant without drawing attention away from the classroom instruction; Provide a positive gesture to support learner actions	Signals must be appropriate and meaningful to be effective and to be viewed as positive gestures to advance learning
Proximity Control	Strategic positioning of the student in the classroom to provide emotional support and/or minimize potential for behavior problems	Increase confidence in own abilities as well as time on task behaviors	Comfort in use of personal space or proximity may vary significantly and must be accommodated to maximize effectiveness
Planned Ignoring	Purposefully ignoring select minor behaviors	Reduce negative behaviors by not drawing attention to or reinforcing them	Ignoring minor undesired behavior is effective if it reduces the behavior and may be a simple means of helping struggling learners deal with RTI curriculum demands
Clearly Articulated Expectations	Providing students with a clear set of directions and steps for learning	Minimize frustration or anxiety due to unfamiliar or confusing academic and behavioral expectations	Many learners require explicit directions and instruction to best meet their academic and social needs; Clear instructions should exist as part of curriculum implementation with fidelity
Planned Physical Movement	Students receive planned opportunities to actively engage in learning activities or tasks through movement within the classroom	Generate active participation in learning and reduce behavior problems associated with extensive passive activities	Supports learners' needs for active learning, planned learning breaks, and ongoing interactions to facilitate progress within RTI models
Student Accountability	Structures allow students to be accountable and responsible for their actions and learning	Students become more aware of their actions and the actions' impacts on their own learning and behaviors	Student accountability in own learning and self-management facilitates greater efficiency in the implementation of multi-tiered curricula within RTI models
Self-Monitoring	Students monitor and evaluate their own learning and behaviors	Encourage positive learning; Increase time on task; Minimize behavior problems	Effective technique for helping students assume greater responsibility for own learning

TABLE 2.2 Study Strategies

Strategy	Task Area	Process	Description
CALL-UP	Notetaking	**C**opy ideas accurately **A**dd necessary details **L**isten and write the question **L**isten and write the answer **U**se text to support notes **P**ut response in own words	Helps students to remain focused on what is happening in class during a note taking task or assignment Helps learners respond more accurately to questions using notes and text to support written responses (Czarnecki, Rosko, & Pine, 1998)
CAN-DO	Acquiring content	**C**reate list of items to learn **A**sk self if list is complete **N**ote details and main ideas **D**escribe components and their relationships **O**verlearn main items, then learn details	Assists with memorization of lists of items through rehearsal techniques
COPS	Writing	**C**apitalization correct **O**verall appearance **P**unctuation correct **S**pelling correct	Provides a structure for proofreading written work prior to submitting it to the teacher
DEFENDS	Improving written expression	**D**ecide on a specific position **E**xamine own reasons for this position **F**orm a list of points explaining each reason **E**xpose position in first sentence of written task **N**ote each reason and associated points **D**rive home position in last sentence **S**earch for and correct any errors	Helps learners defend a particular position in a written assignment
EASY	Studying	**E**licit questions (*who, what, when, where, why*) **A**sk self which information is least difficult **S**tudy easy content first, then difficult content **Y**es—provide self-reinforcement	Helps learners organize and prioritize information by responding to questions designed to identify important content to be learned
FIST	Improving reading comprehension	**F**irst sentence is read **I**ndicate a question about material in first sentence **S**earch for answer to question **T**ie question and answer together through paraphrasing	Helps students actively pursue responses to questions related directly to material being read
GLP	Notetaking	**G**uided **L**ecture **P**rocedure	Provides students with a structure for taking notes during lectures Uses group activity to facilitate effective notetaking
KWL	Reading comprehension	**K**now—document what you know **W**ant to know—document what you want to know **L**earn—list what you have learned	Helps students with reading comprehension and organization of their thoughts, ideas, and acquired knowledge by relating previous knowledge to desired learning (Ogle, 1986)

TABLE 2.2 (Continued)

Strategy	Task Area	Process	Description
MARKER	Time management	**M**ake a list of goals, set the order, set the date **A**rrange a plan for each goal and predict your success **R**un your plans for each goal and adjust if necessary **K**eep records of your progress **E**valuate your progress toward each goal **R**eward yourself when you reach a goal and set a new goal	Helps students effectively use their time by keeping them focused on their goals and reminding them to reward themselves when they reach their goal (Bos & Vaughn, 2006)
NEAT	Writing	**N**ever hand in messy work **E**very paper should be readable **A**lways keep your paper clean **T**ry to remember to put your name and the date on every paper	Assists students to double-check their written work for neatness prior to submission
Panorama	Reading	**P**reparatory stage—identify purpose **I**ntermediate stage—survey and read **C**oncluding stage—memorize material	Includes a three-stage process to assist with reading comprehension
PARS	Reading	**P**review **A**sk questions **R**ead **S**ummarize	Is used with younger students and with those who have limited experiences with study strategies
PENS	Sentence writing	**P**ick a formula **E**xplore different words to fit into the formula **N**ote the words selected **S**ubject and verb selections follow	Helps develop basic sentence structure and helps students write different types of sentences by following formulas for sentence construction
PIRATES	Test taking	**P**repare to succeed **I**nspect instructions carefully **R**ead entire question, remember memory strategies, and reduce choices **A**nswer question or leave until later **T**urn back to the abandoned items **E**stimate unknown answers by avoiding absolutes and eliminating similar choices **S**urvey to ensure that all items have a response	Helps learners to complete tests more carefully and successfully
PQ4R	Reading	**P**review **Q**uestion **R**ead **R**eflect—question how this relates to what you know **R**ecite—talk aloud **R**eview—read over notes and summarize at bottom of page	Helps students to become more discriminating readers

(continued)

TABLE 2.2 Study Strategies (Continued)

Strategy	Task Area	Process	Description
5Rs	Test taking	**R**ecord—take notes on right side of paper **R**educe—write key words, phrases, and questions on left side of paper **R**ecite—talk aloud **R**eflect—question how this relates to what you know **R**eview—read over notes and summarize at bottom of page	Helps students prepare to take tests Helps students clarify and reflect on what they know and how knowledge relates to potential test items
RAP	Reading comprehension	**R**ead paragraph **A**sk self to identify the main idea and two supporting details **P**ut main idea and details into own words	Helps students to learn information through paraphrasing
RARE	Reading	**R**eview selection questions **A**nswer all questions known **R**ead the selection **E**xpress answers to remaining questions	Emphasizes reading for a specific purpose while focusing on acquiring answers to selection questions initially not known
RDPE	Underlining	**R**eview entire passage **D**ecide which ideas are important **P**lan the underlining to include only main points **E**valuate results of the underlining by reading only the underlined words	Helps learners organize and remember main points and ideas in a reading selection by underlining key words
REAP	Reading Writing Thinking	**R**ead **E**ncode **A**nnotate **P**onder	Helps students combine several skills to facilitate discussion about reading material
ReQuest	Reading Questioning	**R**eciprocal **Q**uestioning	Helps students to model teacher questions and receive feedback while exploring the meaning of the reading material
RIDER	Reading comprehension	**R**ead sentence **I**mage (form mental picture) **D**escribe how new image differs from previous sentence **E**valuate image to ensure that it contains all necessary elements **R**epeat process with subsequent sentences	Cues the learner to form a mental image of what was previously learned from a sentence just read
SCORER	Test taking	**S**chedule time effectively **C**lue words identified **O**mit difficult items until end **R**ead carefully **E**stimate answers requiring calculations **R**eview work and responses	Provides a structure for completing various tests by helping students carefully and systematically complete test items

TABLE 2.2 (Continued)

Strategy	Task Area	Process	Description
SOLVE IT	Solving math word problems	**S**ay the problem to yourself **O**mit any unnecessary information in problem **L**isten for key vocabulary terms or indicators **L**isten for key vocabulary terms or indicators **V**ocabulary—change to fit math concepts **E**quation—translate problem into a math equation **I**ndicate the answer **T**ranslate answer back into context of word problem	Assists students to systematically solve math word problems by focusing on key vocabulary in the problem and relating the terms to math concepts and solutions
SQRQCQ	Solving math word problems	**S**urvey word problem **Q**uestion asked is identified **R**ead more carefully **Q**uestion process required to solve problem **C**ompute the answer **Q**uestion self to ensure that the answer solves	Provides a systematic structure for identifying the question identifying the question being asked in a math word problem, computing the response, and ensuring that the question in the problem was answered
SQ3R	Reading	**S**urvey **Q**uestion **R**ead **R**ecite **R**eview	Provides a systematic approach to improve reading comprehension
SSCD	Vocabulary development	**S**ound clues used **S**tructure clues used **C**ontext clues used **D**ictionary used if needed	Encourages students to remember to use sound, structure, and context clues, as well as a dictionary, to address unfamiliar vocabulary
STOP	Writing	**S**uspend judgment (brainstorm) **T**ell thesis **O**rganize ideas **P**lan moves for effective writing	Helps students remember to brainstorm to document potential ideas and generate a thesis statement, document main and subordinate ideas in outline form, and plan foreffective writing (de la Paz,1997)
TOWER	Written reports organization	**T**hink **O**rder ideas **W**rite **E**dit **R**ewrite	Provides a structure for completing initial and final drafts of written reports; may be used effectively with COPS
TQLR	Listening	**T**uning in **Q**uestioning **L**istening **R**eviewing	Assists with listening comprehension by reminding students to generate questions and listen for specific statements related to those questions

(*Study Strategies From Teaching Study Skills to Students with Learning Problems: A Teacher's Guide for Meeting Diverse Needs*, Second Edition (p. 132–136), by J. J. Hoover and J. R. Patton, 2007, Austin, TX: PRO-ED. Copyright 2007 by PRO-ED, Inc. Reprinted with permission.)

Tier 2 instruction must include use of structured EBIs (such as those presented in Chapters 4, 5, and 6). The teaching and behavior management techniques and study strategies presented in Tables 2.1 and 2.2 may be essential in the classroom, but they are NOT Tier 2 interventions.

The practice of skipping the use of EBIs in Tier 2 supplemental instruction, or the misperception that using teaching and behavior techniques or study strategies by themselves represents Tier 2 supplemental instruction, should be avoided.

Figure 2.1 further illustrates the multi-tiered instructional process by relating each of the instructional steps to data collection, which is the topic of the next section.

As shown, when the student data scores indicate that the learner is struggling, the classroom teacher moves along the instructional continuum, making sure to use teaching and behavior management techniques initially, followed by structured EBIs, after which the teacher considers the use of alternate curriculum.

FIGURE 2.1 Continuum of Response-to-Intervention Process for Delivery of Instruction for Struggling Learners

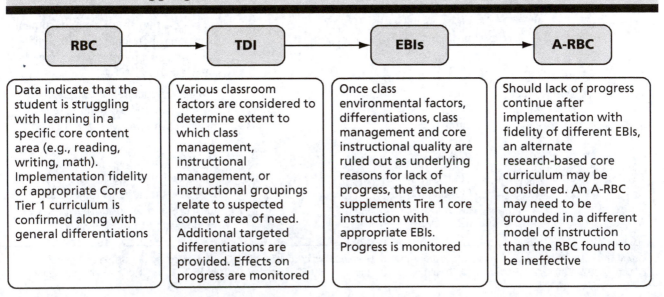

RBC	TDI	EBIs	A-RBC
Data indicate that the student is struggling with learning in a specific core content area (e.g., reading, writing, math). Implementation fidelity of appropriate Core Tier 1 curriculum is confirmed along with general differentiations	Various classroom factors are considered to determine extent to which class management, instructional management, or instructional groupings relate to suspected content area of need. Additional targeted differentiations are provided. Effects on progress are monitored	Once class environmental factors, differentiations, class management and core instructional quality are ruled out as underlying reasons for lack of progress, the teacher supplements Tire 1 core instruction with appropriate EBIs. Progress is monitored	Should lack of progress continue after implementation with fidelity of different EBIs, an alternate research-based core curriculum may be considered. An A-RBC may need to be grounded in a different model of instruction than the RBC found to be ineffective

RBC = Research-Based Curriculum; *TDI* = Targeted Differentiated Instruction; *EBIs* = Evidence-Based Interventions; *A-RBC* = Alternate RBC

Multi-Tiered Assessment Process

Instructional decisions are grounded in an assessment process that, like the instructional process, must be implemented in the proper sequence to be of most value to educators and students. This process is illustrated in the following continuum:

1_____ 2_____ 3_____
  Step 1: Universal Screening   *Step 2:* Progress Monitoring   *Step 3:* Diagnostic

The assessment process is further illustrated in Table 2.3.

TABLE 2.3   Tasks to Implement Assessment in Multi-Tiered Models

Task	Outcome
Tier 1 Assessment Tasks	**Tier 1 Instructional Decisions**
1. Complete universal screening.	Identify at-risk or struggling learners.
2. Confirm Tier 1 instructional fidelity.	Rule out inappropriate or poor instruction.
3. Examine core curriculum and instruction.	Differentiate core curriculum for struggling learners using various teaching and behavior management techniques (Table 2.1), to be implemented for 5–6 weeks.
4. Monitor learner progress every 10–15 school days.	Determine whether differentiations are effective to support adequate progress in Tier 1. (If not, proceed to Tier 2 instruction and assessment procedures.)
Tier 2 Assessment Tasks	**Tier 2 Instructional Decisions**
1. Conduct progress monitoring every 2 weeks.	Document progress during and after an EBI is implemented in a small-group Tier 2 structure for a minimum of 8–10 weeks.
2. Chart or graph the progress monitoring scores.	Visually illustrate learner progress as a result of the EBI.
3. Continue monitoring and charting data scores.	Determine whether Tier 2 instruction is assisting student to make adequate progress. (If not, consider Tier 3 instruction—including alternate curricula.)
Tier 3 Assessment Tasks	**Tier 3 Instructional Decisions**
1. Monitor learner progress weekly.	Document progress during and after intensive intervention is implemented in a pair–small-group Tier 3 structure for a minimum of 10–12 weeks.
2. Chart or graph the progress monitoring scores.	Visually illustrate learner progress as a result of the Tier 3 intervention.
3. Continue monitoring and charting data scores.	Determine whether Tier 3 instruction is assisting student to make adequate progress. (If not, consider referring student to special education.)

As shown in the table, the multi-tiered assessment process primarily emphasizes use of **universal screening** and **progress monitoring** procedures implemented in a systematic and organized manner. Like the *instruction process*, the *assessment process* requires educators to adhere to an organized set of procedures in which screening and progress monitoring occur in integrated ways to provide effective Tiers 1, 2, and 3 levels of instruction. However, there may be unique situations that require deviations from the process, as described in the following section.

ROLE OF DIAGNOSTIC ASSESSMENT ■ Although the primary assessment types in multi-tiered instructional models are universal screening and progress monitoring, diagnostic assessment remains a critical part of the process. Specifically, **diagnostic assessment** assists educators to pinpoint or further clarify learner needs within any tier of instruction (i.e., diagnostic assessment is not only for Tier 3 or special education consideration). For example, an individual diagnostic assessment (e.g., TERA, TOLD) may be needed to pinpoint the specific reading area of need or clarify in the results of the universal screening or progress monitoring, in order to select the most appropriate EBI for a Tier 2 instructional program. A similar scenario is plausible for use of individual diagnostic assessment to develop and implement appropriate Tier 3 interventions for students with more significant needs.

CLEAR INDICATION THAT MORE INTENSIVE INSTRUCTION IS WARRANTED ■ In some instances, the universal screening and/or progress monitoring results clearly indicate that additional implementation of DI through use of teaching and behavior management techniques (presented in Tables 2.1 and 2.2) will be insufficient. In these cases, it may be best to move directly into Tier 2 instruction. Similarly, achievement progress scores may show that more intensive intervention through Tier 3 is warranted, even before there has been an opportunity to collect additional Tier 2 data. Therefore, it is best to carefully balance the implementation, with fidelity, of multi-tiered instruction and assessment with the provision of timely additional instructional supports. This balance is best accomplished by adhering to the processes described in the preceding two sections, holding open the option to move the process along more quickly and/or modify the process to meet more significant needs quickly. Caution must be exercised not to simply skip over any step within either the instructional and assessment processes.

SPECIAL EDUCATION REFERRAL ■ The Council for Exceptional Children (2007) has clearly articulated its position about special education referral and multi-tiered instruction within an RTI framework. Specifically, following due process procedures granted in the Individuals with Disabilities Education Act (IDEA, 2004), the model requires that educators have the option to make a referral to special education at any time within the multi-tiered instructional and assessment process. School teams must honor any referral made and ensure that neither aspects within a multi-tiered model (instructional or assessment) unrealistically prevent timely and appropriate instruction, especially for students who exhibit more significant needs early in the process.

Interpreting Achievement Data Scores

After reading, writing, and mathematics achievement data scores are gathered, the critical task of examining the scores is undertaken. In order to identify a struggling learner, educators need to determine the following:

1. actual versus cut score reflecting expected grade-level proficiency levels
2. gap, if any, between expected and actual levels of proficiency
3. expected and actual rates of progress
4. rate of progress necessary to sufficiently close the gap and achieve at the expected proficiency level.

The universal screening and progress monitoring data indicate current levels of performance. Comparison of current performance levels with that of grade-level peers provides necessary insight into the significance of the data scores. Key elements to examine data scores and expected progress relative to proficiency-level cut scores, gap analysis, and rate of progress are presented next.

Proficiency-Level Cut Scores

Schools or districts establish what is typically referred to as a **cut score**. Students whose scores are below the cut score are considered to be at-risk or struggling. Bender and Shores (2007) suggested that the typical cut score is the 25th percentile, and Hoover (2011b) wrote that a student who is falling below the cut score "may be identified as a struggling learner requiring more intensive instruction (i.e., Tier 2 or 3)" (p. 77). Therefore, one of the initial uses of the screening and monitoring scores is to determine where the scores fall relative to the school's cut score in the targeted academic areas: reading, writing, and mathematics. To this end, charts and graphs should be developed that assist educators to identify and interpret proficiency levels, which, in turn, may be compared with the established cut score.

Gap Analysis

When actual achievement screening or monitoring scores fall below the cut score, additional analysis is required to determine the size of the gap between the expected and actual proficiency-level scores, on the basis of grade level. A simple three-step **gap analysis** procedure may be used to determine the size of the gap (Colorado Department of Education, 2008; Shapiro, 2008):

Step 1: Current Level (CL)—Current level of proficiency is determined (through screening/monitoring scores)

Step 2: Expected Level (EL)—Expected level of proficiency is identified (i.e., average proficiency score according to national or local grade-level norms)

Step 3: Gap—Ratio between current and expected proficiency levels is determined (EL divided by CL = gap)

This "gap analysis" result, in effect, identifies the discrepancy between current and expected achievement levels. Some educators consider a gap score of 2 or greater to be significant and to require immediate Tier 2 instructional adjustments (Colorado Department of Education, 2008). This analysis, in turn, allows teachers to calculate the rate of progress that the student must achieve to "catch up" to peers.

Rate of Progress

Fuchs and Fuchs (1998) stressed the importance using both the expected/actual achievement and expected/actual **rate of progress** scores to best understand the needs of struggling learners. They referred to this as "dual discrepancy" and believe it is important to determine both the gap between proficiency levels and the gap between rates of progress. The following steps identify a learner's rate of progress to achieve growth commensurate with grade-level peers:

1. Identify the level of progress expected of all students in the grade.
2. Establish the time frame that is necessary for the student to achieve at the level expected of all students in the grade (i.e., close the gap).
3. Determine whether the allotted timeframe is sufficient or too aggressive to close the gap.

The following example describes the process for determining the necessary rate of progress, using gap analysis results as found in Hoover (2011b):

Current Performance Level: 25 words per minute

Current Expected Benchmark Performance Level: 65 words per minute (Fall Term)

Gap Analysis: 65 divided by 25 = 2.6 (Gap is significant, over 2.0)

Future Expected Performance Benchmark Level: Students should achieve 95 words per minute by the next monitoring period (Spring Term–15 weeks of instruction)

Expected growth for those achieving Proficiency Benchmark: 95 − 65 = 30 wpm divided by 15 weeks = 2.0 wpm average weekly expected gain for those who make satisfactory progress

Gain Needed by Struggling Learner to Close Gap by Next Monitoring Period: 95 wpm − 25 wpm (current level) = 70 wpm needed to close gap by the Spring Term monitoring

Rate of Progress Required to Close Gap: Spring Term is 15 weeks so learner needs to make an average of 4.6 wpm weekly gain (70 divided by 15 = 4.6) to close the gap between the end of the Fall and Spring Terms compared with an average weekly gain of 2.0 wpm for the typical learner progressing satisfactorily during the same 15-week time period

Growth Timeframe: Typical students making adequate progress will increase their words per minute by 30 (i.e., 65 to 95), making a weekly average increase of 2.0 wpm, whereas our struggling learner must increase by 70 words per minute (25 to 95), making a weekly gain of 4.6 wpm to close the gap by the next monitoring period of 15 weeks

Timeframe Feasibility: The expectation in growth over 15 weeks for the struggling learner is highly aggressive and a more realistic goal should be established. For example, a more realistic progress goal might be to have the learner achieve a 3-wpm gain per week rather than 4.6 wpm.

This gain still represents a 30% increase over that which is expected for the nonstruggling learners. Catching up to the nonstruggling learners will require a 23-week intervention timeframe rather than 15 weeks, which is derived from 3 divided into 70 = 23 weeks.

This decision to adjust the intervention timeframe from a weekly average of 4.6 to 3 wpm is made by the team using data, knowledge, and related assessment information about the struggling learner as well as information about what is expected of nonstruggling students (p. 79).

It is important to bear in mind that the central focus of this text is to assist educators to make the most informed instructional decisions on the basis of achievement universal screening, progress monitoring, and/or diagnostic scores. A complementary theme within this text is that school teams must also gather information about the overall teaching and learning environment that can help interpret the scores. The additional information relates to several essential interrelated curricular elements that exist in all classrooms to provide students DI and sufficient opportunities to learn. Specifically, low data scores only indicate that some aspect in the teaching and learning environment requires change—NOT what needs to be adjusted (Hoover, February 2012, Workshop PowerPoint Presentation, New York City)

A framework for making instructional adjustments that incorporates consideration of achievement data as well as related classroom instruction and management is provided in the next section.

Framework for Making Instructional Adjustments

Several instructional and management elements exist simultaneously in the classroom and one or more of these may require adjustment for a student who is struggling with learning. Educators should consider three important aspects found within Tiers 1, 2, and 3 instruction when they are making **instructional adjustments**. These aspects complement the data interpretation elements that have been discussed (i.e., proficiency scores, gap analysis, rate of progress). These additional considerations are (a) curricular components, (b) classroom management elements, and (c) instructional delivery types.

Curricular Components

Four curricular elements collectively comprise most of what occurs within a classroom. The primary areas found within any teaching environment (i.e., content, process, product) as discussed by Tomlinson (2001) have been expanded by Hoover and Patton (2005) and Hoover (2011a) to further clarify differentiation in the classroom:

- *Content*—Knowledge and skills to be taught and mastered
- *Interventions*—Evidence-based practices to teach content
- *Instructional Arrangement*—Classroom settings used to implement interventions to teach content (i.e., small-group, whole class, paired learning, independent)
- *Class/Instructional Management*—Strategies, routines, expectations, and consequences implemented to facilitate effective instruction to best meet learner needs

These elements are summarized and examined further in Table 2.4.

Each of these curriculum elements is integrated in the teaching and learning environment. As a result, it is essential that school teams consider the role of each element when they are examining screening, monitoring, and diagnostic scores. The interpretation of achievement data scores must take into consideration not only instructional-specific classroom components but also key classroom management elements, in order to ensure that proper differentiations and EBIs are selected.

TABLE 2.4 Classroom and Instructional Curricular Elements

Element	Description	Examples
Content/Skills	Knowledge, skills, ways of thinking, and outcomes learned in mandated state or district curriculum	Investigations Literacy by Design Wilson Foundations
Evidence-Based Interventions (EBIs)	Validated teaching interventions with defined steps, purposes, and described outcomes	Reciprocal Teaching Direct Instruction Collaborative Strategic Reading
Instructional Arrangements	Various small or large groupings, pairs, or independent work arrangements within which students complete assigned tasks	Peer-mediated tasks Small-Group Reading Learning Centers Whole-Class Direct Instruction
Classroom and Instructional Management	Procedures, strategies, and structures used to manage learning and behavior and to create sufficient learning opportunities to meet diverse learning needs in each tier of instruction	Proximity Control Increased Wait Time Consistency Structure/Routines Self-Management

Classroom Management Elements

Meese (2001) identified classroom management as those procedures and practices necessary to structure the learning environment to facilitate learner success. In addition, "good management provides the structure for all learning in the classroom; poor management leads to ineffective learning even if research-based curriculum and evidence-based interventions are implemented properly" (Hoover, 2011b, p. 165). In effect, if achievement data indicate lack of progress, educators should examine the classroom management to make certain it is not the primary reason for the student's struggles. For example, the evidence-based teaching intervention may not need to be changed if poor classroom management exists. Rather, the management procedures should be adjusted and the teaching intervention should remain the same. Table 2.5, developed from classroom management discussions (Hoover & Patton, 2005; Meese, 2001; Sprenger, 2008), illustrates several key classroom areas that school teams should consider to rule out poor management as a primary reason for lack of academic progress.

Educators may use a variety of sources for gathering and documenting evidence pertaining to instruction and classroom management, including observations, work samples, performance-based products, and interviews. A guide titled *Differentiation Quick Screen* (DQS) (Hoover, 2011b) is one tool that may be used to examine each curriculum element relative to the suspected area of need for a struggling learner. (See Form 2.1 at the end of this text.) To ensure that school teams make highly informed decisions about needed

TABLE 2.5   Critical Elements in Classroom Management

Element	Key Components to Consider	Significance to Multi-Tiered Instructional Decisions
Physical Environment	Assigned seating Proximity to teacher Work stations Traffic patterns External stimuli	Physical environmental factors contribute significantly to effective teaching and learning
Classroom Climate	Clear expectations Behavior modeling Demonstrated fairness Self-confidence Maintained emotions Support for positive behaviors	Positive classroom climate promotes effective student interactions, cooperative learning, and achievement growth
Routines and Rules	Posted routines/rules Positive statements Clear expectations Systematic teaching Structured	Clear and consistent class rules and routines are essential to positive classroom management
Reinforcements/Rewards	Antecedents to behaviors Stated consequences Clearly identified rewards Positive praise Demonstrated interest	Consistently implemented reinforcements or rewards in a positive manner contribute significantly to academic achievement
Self-Management	Responsibility Academic ownership Self-control Student accountability	Effective classroom management promotes student ownership of learning, progress, and success
Time Management	Effective use of time Academic learning time Task completion rates	Effective time management is essential for success in today's classrooms due to increased academic expectations
Transitions	Planned movement Sufficient time allocated Transition cues Clear expectations	Effective classroom management includes efficient transitions across activities and subject areas

instructional adjustments, educators should consider the connections among the four curriculum elements. Here is an example of the type of information gathered through use of the DQS for a hypothetical situation and student:

Summary of Current Curriculum Situation and Differentiation Needs

Content/Skills: Jessie, a fifth grader, exhibits similar reading comprehension needs in both oral and silent reading. Jessie possesses sufficient decoding and fluency abilities, which are both strengths to draw on. She also has acquired the skill of answering most literal comprehension questions. Jessie is an English language speaker, and her parents are English speaking as well. Yet she possesses some limitations in her level and usage of oral and receptive language. These limitations affect her ability to complete reading comprehension tasks. When the text is of interest to her, she seems a bit more likely to have higher comprehension; however, Jessie consistently experiences difficulty with inferential comprehension questions.

Evidence-Based Intervention: The content taught within the large-group setting includes primary use of direct instruction. In the small group, it includes use of direct instruction and a degree of differentiation that includes task analysis and scaffolding. The students receive a great deal of modeling and repetition. These techniques are used to meet the goal of helping the students independently comprehend what they read. With the necessary cues and prompts, Jessie responds adequately, especially in the small-group setting. Jessie is not very motivated through use of direct instruction in the large group; however, she is usually motivated if direct instruction is coupled with task analysis and scaffolding procedures. At times, Jessie appears disengaged when she is required to listen to the teacher for more than 5 to 10 minutes at a time. Jessie occasionally participates in whole-group discussions, but she is more likely to contribute when the groups consist of two to four students. She is more likely to acquire the information when it is presented to her in a small group or one-on-one and when she is actively engaged. Attention to the EBI is a factor, as Jessie disengages when she is required to listen for an extended period of time through direct instruction-only methods.

Instructional Arrangement: As mentioned, Jessie is able to attend to reading comprehension tasks within instructional arrangements when she is actively engaged. Also, as mentioned, when Jessie is required to listen for even modest periods of time, she frequently loses focus and begins to look around the room or draw. Jessie works independently when necessary and seems to enjoy tasks that involve writing. However, when she is working independently to attempt tasks, she usually fails to complete reading comprehension assignments, frequently making this arrangement less than productive toward achievement in academic progress. Her peer relations are appropriate, as she is friendly and congenial to everyone in most instructional arrangements. However, Jessie appears somewhat withdrawn at times, especially when she is required to learn in a new social context or large-group setting. The small-group learning arrangement seems to facilitate her ability to acquire information, and within small groups she is more likely to be engaged than in a large-group arrangement. She almost never verbally participates in a general classroom setting of 25 to 30 students unless the students are working in pairs or small groups. In general, Jessie's behaviors are appropriate within the context of a small-group or paired instructional arrangement, a setting that yields more productivity, even though her level of progress with oral and silent reading comprehension is insufficient compared with grade-level expectations.

Class/Instructional Management: The classroom management in Jessie's class includes implementation of consistent rules and routines, clear expectations, smooth transitions, and an overall positive classroom environment. Within this type of classroom, Jessie does very well maintaining self-control. She is not overtly impulsive; in fact, she can show some signs of slightly withdrawn behavior. Jessie uses several sufficient self-management techniques such as organization, working quietly and independently, and paying attention to her tasks. However, she lacks the content skills necessary to correctly complete independent reading comprehension tasks. Therefore, the classroom management facilitates task completion even though Jessie struggles to accurately respond to reading comprehension assignments.

With regard to instructional management, Jessie is provided use of learning centers, direct instruction, scaffolding, and selected differentiations to accommodate her reading comprehension needs. However, when she does not initially understand what is being asked of her, she will not respond at all to any questions, even if subsequent questions are scaffolded. She will sit quietly but will not respond in any way, verbally or nonverbally. This behavior is less likely to occur in a small-group setting than in a large group. As stated, Jessie completes comprehension assignments on time; however, her responses are generally incorrect or incomplete. Jessie struggles to demonstrate certain techniques, such as locating important information, and she has difficulty applying previous experiences to the current content. She requires adjustments to the instructional management to meet her needs.

(Hoover, John J., *Response to Intervention Models: Curricular Implications and Interventions*, 1st Ed., © 2011. Reprinted and Electronically reproduced by permission of Pearson Education, Inc., Upper Saddle River, NJ 07458.)

As illustrated, the screening measure provides educators with valuable information that they need in order to make informed instructional adjustments, along with screening, progress monitoring, and diagnostic data scores.

Instructional Delivery Types

Another critical aspect of interpreting achievement data scores and the related classroom instruction (e.g., DQS information) is the underlying philosophy toward learning in which the instruction is grounded. Although underlying positions may overlap, RBC, EBI, and DI are generally framed around one of three instructional types, as illustrated in Figure 2.2.

FIGURE 2.2   Instructional Delivery Types

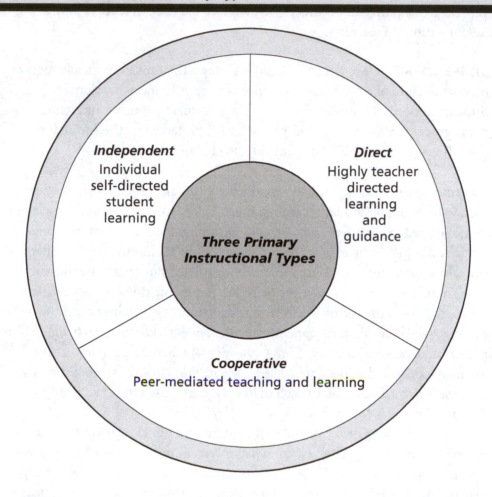

DIRECT ■ Direct instruction includes use of curricula, interventions, and differentiated strategies that require explicit teacher direction, support, and guidance to use in the teaching and learning environment (i.e., teacher-directed learning).

▶ **Selection Basis:** Educators appropriately select and use direct instruction techniques in learning situations when students require a more highly teacher-directed approach to acquire, maintain, and generalize knowledge and skills. Direct instruction is a successful time-tested methodology for teaching in any content area.

COOPERATIVE ■ Many students are provided sufficient opportunities to learn through peer-mediated and related cooperative methodologies. Cooperative-based instruction relies on student-directed learning, personal responsibility, and accountability in school, all completed in collaborative ways (i.e., student group or pair-directed learning)

▶ **Selection Basis:** Cooperative and peer-mediated approaches should be considered when students struggle to make adequate progress with direct instruction and/or as a support to direct instruction to blend both teacher and student—directed learning.

INDEPENDENT ■ Most teaching and learning situations periodically require students to complete tasks on an independent basis to meet a variety of educational needs: (a) enrichment; (b) self-monitoring of task completion, (c) progress monitoring of achievement, or (d) preferred method to reduce distractions (i.e., individual student-directed learning).

▶ **Selection Basis:** Use of independent methods should be purposeful and targeted to best support student learning. Independent methods should be selected when the need to complete tasks, acquire information, or demonstrate application is best achieved by having the students work by themselves, making their own educational decisions rather than relying on decisions made by the teacher.

Therefore, as discussed, a key consideration in making instructional decisions is to determine the most effective instructional type to best meet the learner's needs (i.e., direct, cooperative, independent). Often, a particular EBI is ineffective because educators did not consider whether the primary instructional type provided a "best fit" for the learner. This consideration is directly addressed in the discussion of each of the evidence-based interventions presented in Chapters 4, 5, and 6.

In summary, in order to make effective instructional adjustments, educators must consider (a) achievement data scores, (b) instructional components, (c) classroom management, and (d) instructional delivery types. Collectively, incorporating information from each of these sources provides greater success in (a) providing effective Tier 1 instructional differentiations, thereby reducing the need for Tier 2 supports; (b) selecting and implementing more appropriate and effective Tier 2 supplemental supports, should the learner require more support than can be presented only through Tier 1 instruction; and (c) providing Tier 3 intensive interventions in the most timely and efficient manner possible. In addition, should a special education referral be warranted, all information and data gathered from these collective sources serve to facilitate the most appropriate and informed referral possible.

Universal Screening and Progress Monitoring Example: AIMSweb

Although school districts follow a variety of procedures and processes to gather, chart, and interpret universal screening and progress monitoring data, each school or school system should adhere to some established process to maintain integrity in the standard collection and use of student achievement data scores. One such program that many school systems use for their universal screening and progress monitoring is AIMSweb. This program is summarized here to provide the reader with one example of how to implement the multi-tiered assessment process effectively to gather universal screening and progress monitoring achievement data. The AIMSweb website (www.aimsweb.com) provides more detailed and comprehensive information. The presentation that follows is designed to be general in nature to highlight the process, illustrating one way to implement the assessment process within a multi-tiered instructional model.

Overview of AIMSweb

"AIMSweb is a benchmark and progress monitoring system based on direct, frequent and continuous student assessment" (AIMSweb). AIMSweb includes several topical areas in both academic and behavioral domains. The purpose of this text is to provide interventions and related instructional adjustments in three content areas of reading, writing, and mathematics. The reader is referred to the AIMSweb website and supporting materials for information about the other topical areas emphasized. In addition, this chapter contains an overview of each of these three areas, highlighting key aspects of AIMSweb. For a more detailed discussion and specific instructions for implementing AIMSweb reading, writing, and mathematics, the reader is referred to the sources cited. The remainder of this chapter will provide (a) an overview of the goals and purpose of AIMSweb, and (b) a general structure of AIMSweb for reading, writing, and mathematics.

AIMSweb Goals, Purpose, and Foundation

AIMSweb is a system that supports the formative screening and monitoring of academic and behavioral progress of all learners in grades K–8. Through this system, educators and parents are provided timely data that reflect learner progress in school (Shinn & Shinn, 2002). An overarching goal of AIMSweb is the early identification of learning problems to prevent needs from becoming more severe, including reducing the need for special education referral and placement. Shinn and Shinn (2002) wrote that AIMSweb "informs the instructional process as it occurs by identifying at risk students as early as possible, including those students who are learning and those who are not progressing satisfactorily" (p. 3). A critical purpose of AIMSweb is to determine the extent to which students are learning and progressing within the currently implemented curricula and associated classroom and instructional management.

AIMSweb is grounded in an assessment practice termed curriculum-based measurement (CBM) (Deno, 2005), through which learner progress toward curricular expectations is measured directly against expected curricular benchmarks and learner rate of progress, according to grade level.

CBM provides "reliable, valid, and efficient indicators of academic competence" (Fuchs & Fuchs, 2007, p. 31). CBM includes three types of performances as summarized here (Fuchs & Fuchs, 2007; Hoover, 2011b; Stecker & Lembke, 2005):

> *Mastery Measures* (MM)—MM is an assessment of the student's mastery of individual skills and abilities (e.g., short vowel sounds).
>
> *Skills-Based Measures* (SBM)—SBM is an assessment of individual specific subskills that collectively represent progress in a broader content area. It is a systematic sampling of a mixed set of skills (e.g., various grade-level mathematics problems).
>
> *General Outcome Measure* (GOM)—GOM is an assessment of skills and abilities that reflect grade-level expectations and that require use of several interrelated skills to achieve broad grade-level benchmarks. "General outcome measures are robust indicators of overall achievement" (Stecker & Lembke, 2005, p. 2) (e.g., reading fluency).

CBM is a standardized process for gathering student progress data that was developed and initiated in the 1980s (Deno, 2005) to determine learner growth in core content areas of reading, writing, and mathematics (Fuchs & Fuchs, 2006; Hosp, Hosp, & Howell, 2007). CBM differs from the more traditional end-of-year or summative diagnostic assessment (i.e., Iowa Test of Basic Skills) in several key ways. CBM includes the following qualities (Burns & Gibbons, 2008; Mellard & Johnson, 2008):

- Frequent monitoring of learner progress
- Simple and easy process for administration
- Sensitivity to student progress and growth over short periods of instructional time
- Facilitation of current and timely analysis of learner growth as instruction occurs
- Generation of data scores for use in providing preventative and early intervention services
- Linking of quality of instruction with learner progress on a continuous schedule (e.g., daily, weekly, monthly, three times per year)

A general understanding of the original intent of CBM, including its qualities and components, is essential, as CBM serves as the foundation for AIMSweb. More specifically, CBM originally targeted growth relative to the actual curriculum that is being used in the classroom, increasing assessment–instruction validity. Although this practice remains valuable, broader implications were more limited because it was connected only to the specific curriculum that was being used. In addition, cumulative research on CBM suggests that the direct connection to one curriculum in a specific content area is not necessary if the same standard assessment materials and processes are used to determine progress toward clearly defined skills (Shinn & Shinn, 2002).

Drawing on the extensive research on CBM over several decades, the developers of AIMSweb created screening and monitoring measures that are valid and reliable irrespective of differences associated with various curricula, teachers, classrooms, and schools. A key aspect of AIMSweb that often is not found in the original practice of CBM is the implementation of a standardized set of procedures, both in administration and scoring (Shinn & Shinn, 2002). The standard procedures provide educators increased confidence that assessed learner progress toward defined reading, writing, and mathematics benchmarks is reliable and valid. These assessments provide essential information on which to base needed instructional adjustments.

As a result, AIMSweb provides achievement data that reflect the big picture associated with learner progress in grades K–8, specifically in reading, writing, and mathematics. This emphasis on the GOMs reflects rigorous development, testing, and validation for each topical area emphasized in AIMSweb. Therefore, given its extensive validation and emphasis on GOMs, AIMSweb provides educators with achievement data scores that are gathered within a defined structure as discussed in the following section.

Overview of Structure of AIMSweb

AIMSweb provides two primary types of assessment: (a) benchmark and (b) progress monitoring. The *Benchmark* component includes standardized CBM materials and processes, along with training and web-based data score management for learners in grades K–8 (www.pearsonassessments.com). Benchmarks are completed three times per year for all students, using the three grade-level probes in the content areas of reading, writing, and mathematics. The web-based management provides an effective communication tool that utilizes graphs and charts of student scores illustrating trends, gaps, and associated rates of progress. The *Progress Monitoring* component of AIMSweb provides a series of probes in the same topical areas that are included in the benchmark component, which are designed to be implemented on regular basis (e.g., weekly). The probes for both benchmarking and progress monitoring include short, easy-to-administer assessment measures that may be completed in a few minutes, depending on the topical area and grade level.

As discussed, the CBM process for administering, scoring, and organizing the benchmark and progress monitoring data is standardized to facilitate comparison of scores over time. The following example illustrates the standardized procedures for administering a reading CBM as detailed in Shinn and Shinn (2002, p. 18):

Reading-CBM Standard Directions for One-Minute Administration:

1. Place the unnumbered copy in front of the student.

2. Place the numbered copy in front of you but shielded so the student cannot see what you record.

3. Say: *"When I say 'Begin,' start reading aloud at the top of this page. Read across the page* (DEMONSTRATE BY POINTING). *Try to read each word. If you come to a word you don't know, I'll tell it to you. Be sure to do your best reading. Are there any questions?"* (Pause)

4. Say: *"Begin"* and start your stopwatch when the student says the first word. If the student fails to say the first word of the passage after three seconds, tell them the word, mark it as incorrect, then start your stopwatch.

5. Follow along on your copy. Put a slash (/) through words that the student reads incorrectly.

6. At the end of one minute, place a bracket ( ]) after the last word and say, "Stop."

7. Score and summarize by writing WRC/Errors (WRC = Words Read Correctly).

As illustrated, the administration contains specified procedures and instructions that must be adhered to each time this CBM is administered, in order to ensure standardization. Similar procedures and instructions exist for each of the AIMSweb topical areas (e.g., reading, writing, mathematics), and educators should become proficient with them before they implement this system to students. To facilitate training, AIMSweb staff members provide workshops, webinars, and associated training materials that users will find helpful as they use this system.

By examining AIMSweb data scores relative to cut scores, gap analysis, and rate of progress, educators may make decisions about instructional adjustments that are grounded in several key achievement scores. In addition, when they use data scores in conjunction with other related differentiated classroom and instructional curricula aspects that were discussed in previous sections of this chapter, school teams are best equipped to make the highly informed instructional decisions necessary to select the most appropriate EBIs in reading (see Chapter 4), writing (see Chapter 5), and mathematics (see Chapter 6) while working in collaborative ways (Chapter 3).

CONCLUSION

A multi-tiered instructional process within an RTI framework follows several key steps and adheres to a standard set of procedures. These procedures are designed to ensure that a systematic method exists to screen and monitor learner academic achievement after the structures are properly in place. This chapter presented procedures for the (a) instructional process, (b) assessment process, (c) interpretation of data scores, and (d) application to make informed instructional adjustments. Use of both achievement data scores and documentation of classroom instruction and management was emphasized. An example of one popular and effective method for delivering universal screening and progress monitoring in the schools and classroom was presented (AIMSweb). Collectively, the **multi-tiered process** components discussed in this chapter provide educators with the comprehensive information necessary to deliver informed Tier 1, 2, and 3 instruction to all learners.

Educator: Student: Date:

Instructions: Complete the Quick Screen for Suspected Area of Need:

Grade Level:
Content Area of Need:
Current Level of Proficiency:
Current Rate of Progress:
Gap Analysis Results (Size):
Class Setting in which Need Is Most Frequently Evident:
Primary EBIs:

Using the preceding curriculum needs and setting, check appropriate items within each curriculum component. Check all that apply.

I. Content/Skills—Learner sufficiently possesses the following:
____ Reading level
____ Experiential background
____ Required prerequisite skills
____ Language abilities in language of instruction
____ Motivation to learn and study material
____ Higher-level abstract thinking abilities
____ Other (specify):

II. EBI—Intervention used with learner:
____ Does not lead to learner's progress or attention to task
____ Facilitates active student participation
____ Is an intervention that is clearly understood by the learner
____ Engages the learner by capturing and maintaining his or her attention to the task
____ Is compatible with student preferences toward learning
____ Assists learner to acquire content or skills being taught
____ Other (specify):

III. Instructional Arrangements—Effects of arrangements(s) on learner progress:
Independent Work Setting
____ Independent work is successfully completed
____ Independent work is not successfully completed

Small-Group Setting
____ Facilitates productive learner interactions
____ Leads to completion of assignments or tasks
____ Maintains learner's attention to task
____ Is an appropriate structure for managing learner behaviors
____ Does not lead to learner's progress or attention to task
____ Other (specify):

Large-Group Setting
___ Facilitates productive learner interactions
___ Leads to completion of assignments or tasks
___ Maintains learner's attention to task
___ Is an appropriate structure for managing learner behaviors
___ Does not lead to learner's progress or attention to task
___ Other (specify):

Paired/Cooperative Learning Setting
___ Facilitates productive learner interactions
___ Leads to completion of assignments or tasks
___ Maintains learner's attention to task
___ Is an appropriate structure for managing learner behaviors
___ Does not lead to learner's progress or attention to task
___ Other (specify):

IV. **Classroom/Instructional Management—Effects of management procedures on learner's curriculum area of need:**
Relative to learner's curriculum need(s), the classroom management facilitates
___ Self-management of behavior
___ Student's responsibility for own learning
___ Positive physical and emotional environment
___ Structured, periodic movement within classroom
___ Efficient time management
___ Smooth transitions
___ Differentiation to meet social or behavioral needs
___ Effective use of academic learning time
___ Relevant and meaningful rewards and reinforcement
___ Consistency in implementation of class rules and routines
___ Sufficient opportunities to learn
___ Implementation of class management techniques with fidelity
___ Other (specify):

Relative to learner's curriculum need(s), the instructional management facilitates
___ Effective uses of student groupings
___ Proper uses of independent learning
___ Effective uses of learning centers
___ Differentiation to meet academic needs
___ Learner's activation and application of prior knowledge
___ Valuing cultural diversity in teaching
___ Accommodating language needs and levels of proficiency
___ Appropriate use of direct instruction methodology
___ Use of cooperative learning
___ Implementation of instructional techniques with fidelity
___ Sufficient progress toward curricular benchmarks in content/skill area(s)
___ Other (specify):

(continued)

Summary of Current Curriculum Situation and Differentiation Needs

Content/Skills:

EBI:

Instructional Arrangement:

Class/Instructional Management:

(J. J. Hoover. (2011b). *Response to intervention: Curricular implications and interventions* (pp. 23–26). Upper Saddle River, NJ: Pearson/Allyn & Bacon. Reprinted with permission.)

CHAPTER 3

Collaboration to Implement Instructional Adjustments

▶ Chapter Overview

THE COMBINATION OF VARIED needs, limited time, and necessary expertise presents educators with a tremendous challenge as they make instructional adjustments within multi-tiered instructional models. Collaboration is a time-tested process that provides educators opportunities to simultaneously meet learner needs that are associated with DI, Tiers 1 and 2 instruction, ongoing progress monitoring, and overall increased accountability. This chapter includes discussion of strategies for collaborating to meet the needs of all students. The strategies draw on the collective expertise of a variety of educators, including general and special educators, interventionists, and other relevant support personnel. Achievement data serve as the foundation for making instructional adjustment decisions and collaborative expertise serves as the foundation for successfully selecting and implementing those adjustments. We also discuss process for building collaboration within the school decision-making team structure, along with key contributions that various educators provide in a professional collaboration environment.

- ▶ Collaboration model
- ▶ Team collaboration
- ▶ Collaboration roles
- ▶ Collaborative knowledge expertise
- ▶ Facilitating change

INTRODUCTION

One reality in today's teaching and learning environments is an increase in student expectations within highly defined time constraints. Doing more with less time is becoming the norm rather than the exception for most classroom teachers. In addition, as delivery of multi-tiered models continue to expand within our nation's schools, demands on educators' time increases as universal screening, progress monitoring, and multi-tiered instruction are implemented. Implementation of a multi-tiered model requires necessary changes to be made in our schools and classrooms, eventually leading to the need to make instructional adjustments for all learners to ensure that high-quality teaching is implemented with fidelity. Although most educators are equipped to address some of these challenges, few if any are capable of satisfactorily addressing all these expectations by themselves.

One of the best solutions to meeting these and other contemporary instructional demands is for educators to collaborate to gather academic achievement data, organize the results, interpret the scores and information, develop meaningful instructional adjustments, and subsequently implement needed changes in the classroom. Many ideas and concepts are associated with collaboration. The three elements that are most relevant to discussions here are (a) the collaboration model, (b) factors associated with change, and (c) collaboration roles. Each of these topics is presented in the sections that follow, providing a collaborative framework for effectively applying the concepts, processes, and interventions discussed in the other chapters of this text.

Collaboration Model

Collaboration involves several interrelated skills and abilities implemented within a process that brings colleagues together cooperatively to meet the needs of all learners. The collaborative model discussed in this section supports the collective decision-making process within the overall school team efforts. That is, effective collaboration contributes significantly to the efficient and effective operations of the decision-making team.

TABLE 3.1 Collaborative Areas of Expertise in Multi-Tiered Models

Expertise Area	Overview	Decision-Making Skills
1. Underlying Knowledge Base	Key elements connected to effective instruction and assessment	Data collection procedures Data interpretation Differentiated classroom Classroom management Universal screening Progress monitoring
2. Interaction Skills	Problem-solving and communication skills for effective interactions	Professional respect Active listening Consensus making Objectivity Professional trust Constructive feedback
3. Intrapersonal Attitudes	Personal beliefs and behaviors brought to the collaborative process	Respect for cultural identity Professional integrity Ability to take risks Creativity Self-sufficiency Proactive thinking

Collaborative Knowledge Expertise

Idol (2002) identified three areas of competence that educators should possess in order to be effective collaborators. The identified areas of expertise, as applied to multi-tiered instructional decision making, are described in Table 3.1. Educators who are competent in the three identified areas possess the necessary skills for effective collaboration to occur.

As shown, the three collaborative areas of expertise provide a strong foundation for educators to work cooperatively to

1. gather necessary screening and progress-monitoring achievement data (e.g., through AIMSweb).

2. examine classroom and instructional management elements in the teaching and learning environment (e.g., DQS).

3. interpret data scores and related instructional information.

4. generate an informed decision concerning necessary instructional adjustments.

5. implement the recommended instructional adjustments.

The extent to which each member of the decision-making team possesses the abilities in the table is the extent to which the group has the best chance to succeed with instructional decision-making in collaborative ways. However, although the abilities provide the foundation for effective collaboration, an established process to which all educators adhere provides the mechanism for utilizing those abilities in the best possible ways to help all learners. For additional information about these three foundational areas of expertise, see Idol (2002).

Collaborative Model Elements

A common theme among the various collaborative models, processes, and components is that supportive efforts among educators can meet diverse needs of all learners. Although most educators agree that some form of collaboration improves the success of learners, "collaborative relationships in schools, however, are difficult to develop and even more challenging to maintain" (Walther-Thomas, Korinek, & McLaughlin, 2005, p. 183). These authors state further that lack of adequate resources and professional development, along with competing priorities, inhibit the best intentions of educators who wish to collaborate. To address these and related challenges, we present six collaborative model elements in Figure 3.1, reflecting discussions

FIGURE 3.1   Components of Team Collaboration

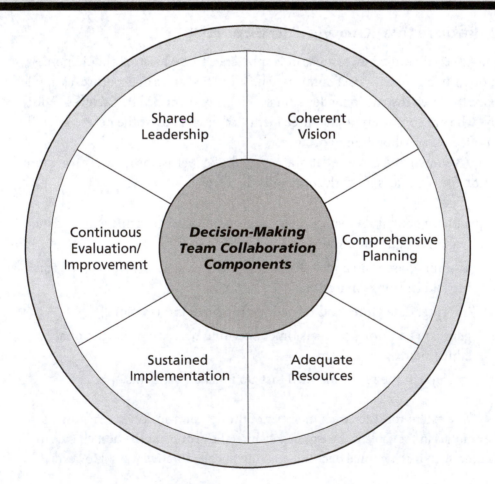

provided by Walther-Thomas, Korinek, and McLaughlin (2005). Each of these elements is briefly discussed and the reader is referred to this source for additional information.

SHARED LEADERSHIP ■ Collaboration requires shared decision making and discussion among team members to generate ownership. The team should share the leadership in the interpretation of instructional data, generation of instructional adjustments, and implementation of those recommended adjustments in the classroom.

COHERENT VISION ■ To minimize competing priorities, a collaborative team agrees on a vision and purpose. The school team members should articulate a vision for the team soon after the team is formed, and future discussions and decisions should fall within the parameters of that vision.

COMPREHENSIVE PLANNING ■ After the vision has been determined, collaborators should collectively generate key items that are necessary to successfully implement the vision (e.g., achievement data collection, classroom and instructional management considerations, gap analysis, rate of progress). Plans should be developed for the most efficient and effective ways to gather data and related instructional information, drawing on the collaborative efforts of various team members.

ADEQUATE RESOURCES ■ Collaboration will be more successful if the team members are provided sufficient resources and support to carry out their responsibilities. Perhaps the most important resource after principal and district support is adequate time to collaborate to examine, discuss, and make decisions about struggling learners.

SUSTAINED IMPLEMENTATION ■ Collaboration by its very nature involves different individuals with different perceptions about the same student need or situation, which may result in differences of opinion regarding data interpretation, instructional adjustments, and classroom implementation. Team members must understand this reality from the beginning of the collaborative efforts and be committed to working through their differences, keeping in mind the "shared vision." By remaining focused on the tasks at hand and respecting the "shared leadership" element, teams sustain their collaborative spirit over the long term, even as members come and go from the team.

CONTINUOUS EVALUATION AND IMPROVEMENT ■ As educators, we are all too familiar with assessment and evaluation. Any collaboration structure also needs continuous evaluation and ongoing enhancements. Therefore, the last collaborative element is the initiation of a simple process to evaluate team collaboration and help make informed instructional decisions and adjustments for all learners.

The six collaborative elements address the primary areas that are needed in order for successful collaboration to occur. Form 3.1, *Guide for Collaborative Model Elements*, which is included at the end of this chapter, provides team members an informal way to monitor the use and implementation of each element, which in turn provides one means for continuous evaluation of team collaboration. Application of the three collaborative areas of expertise, combined with the six collaboration model elements, provides a solid foundation for successful multi-tiered instructional decision making.

Facilitating Change

An inevitable result of increased emphasis on universal screening and progress monitoring within multi-tiered instruction is the need for educators to **facilitate change** to implement these required model components. In addition, the increased emphasis on quality of instruction rather than intrinsic disorders requires educators to change the way they view teaching and learning, especially for struggling learners. As a result, an understanding of the change process and potential challenges assists educators to make necessary adjustments in a more efficient and effective manner.

Change Process

In discussing the transition to multi-tiered instruction within an RTI framework, Hall (2008) wrote that schools should only undertake this task after careful thought and consideration of needed supports and changes. It is best when change occurs within a collaborative model, as indicated by Batsche, Curtis, Dorman, Castillo, and Porter (2007), who wrote "all primary stakeholders must be involved in every stage of the change process" (p. 379). In support, Hoover (2011b) discussed five elements that should be considered as change is implemented:

1. *Change Awareness*—Those involved in the change must initially see the possibility that effective change can occur.

2. *Change Interest*—Those involved in the change must have an interest in creating and implementing the change.

3. *Time for Change*—Educators involved in the change must be provided sufficient time to consider the change so that they can evaluate its feasibility, appropriateness, and potential value for its intended purpose.

4. *Initial Implementation*—Aspects of the change initially should be implemented on a limited scale to allow educators to work out specific details,

identify potential challenges that arise, resolve the challenges, and refine the change to best facilitate widespread implementation.

5. *Full Implementation*—Using the results obtained from the initial and controlled-scale implementation, the change is subsequently completed on a full-scale basis. At this time the full change is completed and its effectiveness is documented and evaluated to allow educators to continuously enhance the process and ensure its continued success.

Weiner (2003) wrote that effective change involves use of problem-solving, collaboration, and increased learning, resulting in positive personal growth. Therefore, the professional growth coupled with the collaborative model presented in the previous section combine to facilitate the initiation and institution of effective change, especially when the five change elements are valued in the process.

In addition to these change elements, several qualities of change should be embedded into the process to ensure its effectiveness (Hoover & Patton, 2005):

- Change happens to and directly affects individuals.
- Change occurs as a process rather than a single event.
- The same change is perceived differently by educators in different roles. (For example, a school psychologist, general classroom teacher, and reading interventionist may all view the change differently.)
- The actual implementation of the change is influenced by different events or factors, some of which are not under the control of people who are implementing or directly affected by the change.
- Change is a process that may be facilitated and guided to achieve its objective(s).

Fixsen, Naoom, Blasé, and Wallace (2007) wrote that the ultimate goal of engaging individuals in change is to increase one's capacity to deal with and accept change, rather than simply expecting surface-level, short-term change. Facilitating and further developing the capacity for change makes it easier to address future changes and implement them with improved chances for success over the long term. These change qualities are especially relevant to educators who are engaged in making the transition from the previous prereferral model to the contemporary multi-tiered instructional practices.

Collaboration Roles and Skill Sets

In addition to possessing abilities within the three key areas of expertise that we have discussed (i.e., Knowledge Base, Interaction Skills, Intrapersonal Attitudes), collaboration requires educators to develop skills that reflect the key roles they must assume to best meet the needs of all learners. In a review of literature, Hoover and Patton (2008) identified several primary skill sets that are most relevant for educators of struggling students. These skill sets were discussed relative to the role of special education teachers in multi-tiered models; however, they apply to any educator (e.g., general educators, interventionists, remedial class teachers, bilingual/ESL teachers). Four of these roles are presented here with specific emphasis on helping educators acquire a broad-based understanding of each area to best facilitate collaboration among educators. The four roles, along with selected associated skill sets adapted from Hoover and Patton (2008) and Hoover (2011b), are presented in Table 3.2. The table is followed by a discussion of the significance of these roles relative to making data-based adjustments in implementing Tiers 1, 2, and 3 instruction. The skill sets presented are critical abilities associated with each of the four roles.

As shown, a variety of skill sets are necessary to successfully implement the four collaborative roles. The roles and the skill sets are not all-inclusive and more may be added. The roles selected directly reflect the primary expectations that are associated with the implementation of a multi-tiered instructional model; the selected skill sets reflect key components associated with each of the roles.

Collaboration among educators who have sufficient knowledge and skills in each of the four roles provides students sufficient opportunities to learn. Form 3.2, *Collaboration Roles Self-Evaluation Guide*, which is found at the end of the chapter, provides a guide for educators to use to self-evaluate their proficiency with subskills found within each of the four roles as summarized here:

> *Data-Based Decision Maker*—Members of school teams that base instructional decisions on achievement screening and progress monitoring data scores are challenged to accurately interpret the results within the overall classroom and instructional management structures. The skill sets identified in Table 3.2 reflect key elements that facilitate accurate interpretation of achievement and associated instructional information.
>
> *Implementer of Evidence-Based Practice*—An ultimate outcome in the collection of achievement data is to select and implement needed instructional adjustments (in, e.g., reading, writing, mathematics). Linking achievement data scores with the struggling learner's classroom atmosphere and instructional evidence-based practices provides school teams a comprehensive overview of the needs of all students. This information, in turn, provides a solid foundation for selecting and implementing EBIs such as those presented in Chapters 4, 5, and 6. Knowledge of the process for delivering evidence-based practices is essential to ensure fidelity of the instructional adjustments. Therefore, a key quality in successful collaboration is that all educators know and understand the evidence-based practices, whether they implement them themselves or collaborate to assist others with their implementation.

TABLE 3.2   Collaboration Roles and Associated Skill Sets

Collaborative Role	Skill Sets—Knowledge
Data-Based Decision Maker	Achievement Data Collection Procedures
	Gap Analysis Formula
	Rate of Progress Norms
	Problem-Solving Abilities
	CBM
	Data Charting/Graphing Methods
	Assessment Validity and Reliability
	Instructional Management Assessment
	Process to Confirm Instructional Fidelity
	Universal Screening Purposes
	Effective Communication
Implementer of Evidence-Based Practice	Evidence-Based Reading Interventions
	Evidence-Based Writing Interventions
	Evidence-Based Mathematics Interventions
	Process to Confirm Fidelity of Evidence-Based Practices
	Direct Instruction
	Task Analysis
	Precision Teaching
	Mastery Learning
	Culturally Responsive Instruction
	Research-Based Curriculum (RBC)
Implementer of Positive Behavior Supports Program	Applied Behavior Analysis (ABA)
	Antecedent/Behavior/Consequence (ABC)
	Functional Behavior Assessment Process
	Classroom Management Assessment
	Self-Management Strategies
	Behavior Intervention Plan (BIP)
	Differentiated Behavior Management Strategies
	Interaction between classroom academic and behavioral expectations, needs, and outcomes
	Academic needs associated with social-emotional/behavioral needs
Expertise in Differentiating Instruction	Sheltered Instruction
	Study Skills
	Learning Strategies
	Scaffolding
	Classroom/Instructional Management Strategies
	Differentiated Instructional Management Strategies
	Academic Learning Time
	Differentiated Classroom
	Universal Design for Learning (UDL)
	Co-teaching Skills

Implementer of Positive Behavior Supports—Although the emphasis in this text is on the three academic areas of reading, writing, and mathematics, inherent within any effective instructional decision is the need to consider the student's social-emotional and behavioral needs to more completely understand the learner's academic needs. As a result, collaboration among educators requires the educators to have knowledge and skills associated with the school's positive behavior supports program and to understand how the program is implemented at the classroom level for students who are struggling with learning. A school's positive behavior supports program provides school teams with essential information to support academic decision making that is grounded in achievement screening and progress monitoring data scores.

The interrelationship between academics and behavior is strong and it is often difficult to separate the two to make the best instructional decisions. For example, educators must decide whether a struggling learner's achievement problem is associated most with the classroom management, instructional intervention, grouping of students, or some other aspect in the teaching and learning environment. The influences of classroom and instructional management on a learner's academic progress were discussed in detail in Chapter 2, highlighting the importance of examining the interconnected elements of instructional interventions, classroom behavior management, instructional management, and progress-monitoring processes and strategies. Most learner problems in school affect academic performance; however, as previously emphasized, associated classroom and instructional management elements may directly affect students' academic progress, requiring instructional adjustments that may not need to include changing the instructional intervention. Within the overall achievement data collection and analysis procedures for the core areas of reading, writing, and mathematics, educators should also examine social, emotional, and behavioral aspects associated with the suspected need (e.g., behaviors exhibited during reading instruction or during a small-group writing activity). This examination may include completion of a functional behavioral assessment, classroom observations, interviews, the DQS described in Chapter 2, or other related information-gathering tasks that are designed to pinpoint social-emotional or behavioral needs associated with the academic need. For additional information on positive behavioral support, the reader is referred to Johnson, Carter, and Pool (2010).

Provider of Differentiating Instruction—The ability to differentiate instruction is essential to any multi-tiered instructional model. In many decision-making meetings about instructional adjustment, it is helpful to examine and confirm the manner and extent to which learners are provided differentiated instruction within an overall differentiated classroom. School team members must be proficient in differentiated teaching and learning so that they may best contribute to academic achievement data score discussions. Therefore, a critical role within collaboration is the ability to identify and assist others to use appropriate classroom and instructional differentiations, such as those presented in Tables 2.1 and 2.2.

CONCLUSION

The significance of collaboration to implement instructional adjustments cannot be overstated, as it serves as the foundation for putting into action the decisions made by the school decision-making teams. The supports that team members provide to one another through collaboration ensure sufficient opportunities to learn for all students as educators share their roles, responsibilities, expertise, and supports. Collaboration is essential, especially given the time constraints often associated with balancing the need for (a) documenting, examining, and applying screening and monitoring achievement data and information; (b) making instructional adjustment decisions; and (c) implementing the instructional adjustments. Adhering to a structured process for collaborating, such as the one presented in this chapter, ensures that necessary supports are identified and provided to all educators and students. In addition, becoming proficient in each of the four collaboration roles discussed in this chapter ensures that educators grow professionally, make valued contributions, and improve the collaboration process.

FORM 3.1   Guide for Evaluating Elements of Collaboration

Instructions: Rate the extent to which each collaboration element is implemented in the school team decision-making process. Provide relevant comments to clarify ratings.

1—Little or none	2—To some degree	3—Regularly	4—Extensively

Collaboration Element		Rating		
Shared Leadership (Each member is involved in the decision) *Comments:*	1	2	3	4
Coherent Vision (Vision is established and discussions/decisions fall within the vision) *Comments:*	1	2	3	4
Comprehensive Planning (Action plan to implement the vision is developed and the decision-making process adheres to it) *Comments:*	1	2	3	4
Adequate Resources (Team is provided adequate resources to implement its vision and action plan) *Comments:*	1	2	3	4
Sustained Implementation (Team remains focused on implementing its vision and action plan by avoiding off-target discussions) *Comments:*	1	2	3	4
Continuous Evaluation/Improvement (Ongoing team evaluation and improvements occurs) *Comments:*	1	2	3	4

(Hoover, John J., *Response to Intervention Models: Curricular Implications and Interventions*, 1st Ed., © 2011. Reprinted and Electronically reproduced by permission of Pearson Education, Inc., Upper Saddle River, NJ 07458.)

FORM 3.2   Collaboration Roles Self-Evaluation Guide

Teacher: _____   Date: _____

Instructions: Rate each item to reflect your current level of proficiency using the following scale:

1 = Not Proficient   2 = Little Proficiency
3 = Some Proficiency   4 = Highly Proficient

I. Data-Driven Decision Maker

__ Achievement Data Collection Procedures
__ Gap Analysis Formula
__ Rate of Progress Norms
__ Problem-Solving Abilities
__ Curriculum-Based Measurement
__ Data Charting/Graphing Methods
__ Assessment Validity and Reliability
__ Instructional Management Assessment
__ Process to Confirm Tier 1/2 Instructional Fidelity
__ Universal Screening Purposes
__ Effective Communicator
__ Progress-Monitoring Procedures

Summary of Proficiency with Data-Driven Decision Making:

II. Implementer of Evidence-Based Practice

__ Evidence-Based Reading Interventions
__ Evidence-Based Writing Interventions
__ Evidence-Based Mathematics Interventions
__ Process to Confirm Fidelity of Evidence-Based Practices
__ Direct Instruction
__ Precision Teaching
__ Mastery Learning
__ Task Analysis
__ Culturally Responsive Instruction
__ Other (Specify):

Summary of Proficiency with Evidence-Based Practice:

III. Implementer of Positive Behavior Supports

___ Applied Behavior Analysis (ABA)
___ Antecedent/Behavior/Consequence (ABC)
___ Functional Behavior Assessment Process
___ Self-Management Strategies
___ Classroom Behavior Management
___ Classroom Management Assessment
___ Behavior Intervention Plan (BIP)
___ Differentiated Behavior Management Strategies
___ Interaction between Classroom Academic and Behavioral Expectations, Needs, and Outcomes
___ Academic Needs associated with Social-Emotional and Behavioral Needs
___ Other:

Summary of Proficiency with Positive Behavior Supports Implementation:

IV. Provider of Differentiated Instruction

___ Classroom Instructional Management
___ Differentiated Instructional Management Strategies
___ Instructional Management Assessment
___ Sheltered Instruction
___ Scaffolding
___ Study and Learning Strategies
___ Time on Task and Academic Learning Time
___ Cultural and Linguistic Diversity Roles in Education
___ Academic Learning Time
___ Differentiated Classroom
___ Universal Design for Learning (UDL)
___ Co-teaching Skills
___ Other:

Summary of Proficiency with Differentiating Instruction:

PART II

Reading, Writing, and Mathematics Interventions

CHAPTER 4

Evidence-Based Reading Practices

▶ Chapter Overview

Nᴜᴍᴇʀᴏᴜs ʀᴇsᴇᴀʀᴄʜ ᴀɴᴅ ᴇᴠɪᴅᴇɴᴄᴇ-ʙᴀsᴇᴅ practices exist to address needs that are associated with key reading abilities assessed through screening and progress monitoring. These practices include (a) differentiated teaching strategies, (b) research-based comprehensive reading curricula, and (c) evidence-based reading interventions. This chapter provides practical information about each of these three areas, with detailed presentations of several of the more widely used and effective evidence-based reading interventions for learners who are at-risk or struggling. The EBIs are followed by an overview of some of the more widely used comprehensive research-based reading curricula to teach struggling readers, along with numerous, easily implemented teaching strategies to provide differentiated instruction within the Tier 1 core reading curriculum.

The focus, however, of this chapter is the evidence-based reading interventions. Several selected program and instructional interventions are presented in a manner that enables readers to apply them in Tiers 1 and 2 reading instruction in conjunction with and supplemental to the implementation of general class differentiations (i.e., teaching strategies) and the Tier 1 core reading curricula (i.e., research-based comprehensive reading curricula).

► Evidence-based reading interventions
► Research-based reading programs
► Teaching and student strategies
► Foundations of reading instruction

Reading Content Areas and Multi-Tiered Instructional Interventions

Early Literacy/Reading

Select an early literacy/reading intervention that targets the assessed content area in which the learner demonstrates inadequate reading progress.

	Early Literacy	Reading: ORAL READING FLUENCY (ORF)	MAZE (Silent Comprehension)
READING INTERVENTION			
Reciprocal Teaching			X
Classwide Peer Tutoring (CWPT)		X	X
Language Experience Approach (LEA)	X		
Reading Response Journal			X
Literature Response Groups (LRGs)			X
Graphic Organizers			X
Collaborative Strategic Reading (CSR)			X
Peer-Assisted Learning Strategies (PALS)		X	X
Fernald Multisensory Approach	X		
Self-Questioning			X
Reader's Theater		X	X
Incremental Rehearsal		X	

INTRODUCTION

The selection and use of **evidence-based reading interventions** is the foundation of delivering effective multi-tiered instruction for struggling readers in each tier or level. After screening and/or progress monitoring reading data that indicate an at-risk or struggling learner, classroom teachers and school teams must adjust instruction to best meet the student's reading needs. Should the student's achievement data and supporting supplemental classroom and instructional evidence indicate the need to adjust the reading intervention, educators should identify an evidence-based practice and appropriately implement it in the classroom. We begin with an overview of the foundation of effective reading instruction, which includes the gathering of screening and progress-monitoring data. The interpretation of these data leads to the selection of appropriate reading interventions.

Foundations of Reading Instruction

For decades, researchers have theorized about the most effective programs (e.g., basal, linguistics, whole language) and types of interventions (e.g., phonics, whole word, direct, cooperative) for helping learners to develop and master the skill of reading. One of the most recent efforts to clarify which necessary reading components to include in effective reading instruction was undertaken by the National Reading Panel (NRP, 2000). The report completed by the members of this panel summarized findings about the skills that are necessary for effective reading development, as determined through an extensive review of research studies spanning three decades. Five components were identified in the NRP report as essential to effective reading instruction and programming. These elements are summarized in Table 4.1, which was developed from information found in Ehri (2006); Klingner and Geisler (2008); Mercer, Mercer, and Pullen (2011); and NRP (2000).

TABLE 4.1 Five Essential Elements to Effective Reading Instruction

Reading Essential Element	Description
Phonological Awareness	Skills necessary to identify and use specific elements of spoken language, including phonemes, syllables, and words. Phonemic awareness is a subset of phonological awareness and emphasizes recognition of individual sounds (i.e., phonemes).
Alphabetic Principle/Phonics	An understanding of sound–symbol relationships and skills for combining sounds into words, specifically acquiring knowledge about the relationship between written letters and spoken sounds.
Fluency	Skills necessary to apply word recognition and comprehension to read quickly and accurately with expression. Fluent readers are able to collectively use various reading subskills, including phonemic awareness, letter naming, and sound–symbol relationships.
Vocabulary	The words a learner acquires in communication reflect one of two primary types of vocabulary: oral and reading. Oral vocabulary includes listening and speaking, and reading vocabulary involves print and writing. Much of vocabulary is acquired through daily experiences (e.g., being read to, looking at reading material, making verbal conversations, reading aloud). However, some vocabulary development requires direct teaching through modeling, practice, and use of strategies.
Comprehension	Understanding reading material reflects comprehension as learners interact with text. Comprehension is a complex process that requires direct teaching of cognitive strategies in order for students to construct meaning from written material.

Reading Interventions

The discussions that follow provide readers with key reading EBIs that may be used to meet identified reading needs, particularly in the areas of fluency, comprehension, vocabulary development, and motivation. Although this list is not all-inclusive, the interventions selected are frequently used in today's classrooms and have been shown to be effective through extensive research. Use of these interventions should occur to meet needs of struggling readers. As discussed in Chapter 2, educators should implement these reading EBIs in conjunction with Tier 1 instruction in the general class setting, followed by their use in supplemental Tier 2 support as necessary, and PRIOR to using different or alternative curricula. The descriptions for each intervention were developed from numerous sources cited in the discussions that follow; the reader is referred to these sources for additional information. The purpose here is to present each evidence-based reading intervention in sufficient detail to guide practitioners in the selection and use of each on the basis of the learner's screening or progress-monitoring results and related instructional evidence.

Table 4.2 provides a listing of the interventions presented in this chapter, which includes primary instructional type (e.g., direct, cooperative,

TABLE 4.2   Reading Evidence-Based Interventions**

Reading Intervention	Primary Instructional Type	Primary Targeted Reading Area(s)
Reciprocal Teaching	Direct	Comprehension
Classwide Peer Tutoring (CWPT)	Cooperative	Fluency; Comprehension
Language Experience Approach	Direct	Emergent Skills; Readiness
Read Naturally Strategy	Independent	Fluency; Phonics
Reading Response Journal	Independent	Comprehension; Motivation
Literature Response Groups	Cooperative	Comprehension; Motivation
Graphic Organizers	Direct	Vocabulary; Concept Development
Collaborative Strategic Reading	Cooperative	Content Area Comprehension
Peer-Assisted Learning Strategies	Cooperative	Fluency; Comprehension
Fernald Multisensory Approach	Direct	Vocabulary; Emergent Skills
Self-Questioning	Independent	Comprehension
Reader's Theater	Cooperative	Fluency; Comprehension
Incremental Rehearsal	Direct	Fluency; Vocabulary
Reading Recovery	Direct	Emergent Skills

**Note: Read Naturally and Reading Recovery are reading programs that include highly useful and generalizable steps and strategies. These two selected programs are described here to highlight their intervention qualities; programs are also summarized in a subsequent section.

independent) and the primary reading skill area(s) that the intervention targets. Although some of the interventions use more than one instructional type (e.g., direct and independent), the table and subsequent discussions highlight the primary instructional type used within the intervention, with the recognition that the intervention may also include a secondary instructional type. The selected reading interventions may be initially used in conjunction with Tier 1 core curricula as well as for supplemental Tier 2 instruction; most require little formal technical training. Also, most interventions do not require additional curriculum materials, so they easily fit into the existing Tier 1 core reading curriculum and instruction.

Intervention: *Reciprocal Teaching*

Primary Instructional Type	Primary Target Population	Primary Targeted Content Area(s)
_X_ Direct ___ Cooperative ___ Independent	The primary target population is sixth graders through ninth graders; this intervention may also be used in upper elementary and secondary grades.	The primary target is reading comprehension.

INTERVENTION OVERVIEW ■ Reciprocal Teaching (Palincsar & Brown, 1984) is an intervention in which a teacher and a small group of students explore reading comprehension. Following teacher guidance and direction, students use four comprehension strategies: Questioning, Summarizing, Clarifying, and Predicting. Reciprocal Teaching was initially designed for use with junior high school learners who possessed adequate decoding skills yet needed to develop their comprehension skills. Since its inception, this intervention has been expanded for use with larger groups of learners and elementary students. When it is used with younger students, the "dialogue" aspect is preceded by explicit instruction to teach the cognitive strategies that students employ in order to engage in discussion. These strategies are associated with the four comprehension skills (Rosenshine & Meister, 1994). The underlying premise of reciprocal teaching is to address the four types of comprehension skills through dialogue in collaborative groups (with teacher guidance and support). The dialogue experience helps to "bring meaning to the text while helping [learners] internalize the use of the strategies, thus, ultimately improving their reading comprehension" (Hoover et al., 2008, p. 198).

INSTRUCTIONAL USAGE ■ Reciprocal Teaching is used when the goal is to improve reading comprehension through small-group instruction with teacher-directed guidance. This intervention is appropriate for use with elementary and middle school students who are capable of learning through dialogue, explicit teaching, and guided learning in small- or large- group situations.

RESEARCH-BASED EVIDENCE ■ Reciprocal Teaching is grounded in three research-based foundations: (a) zone of proximal development (Vygotsky, 1978), in which the emphasis is placed on student learning through social interaction and guidance rather than independent learning; (b) scaffolding, in which students are provided adjustable and temporary learning supports to complete tasks or solve problems they would not have been able to complete otherwise; and (c) teacher-guided instruction (building on the first two items), with emphasis on challenging learner expectations (Palincsar & Brown, 1989). Researchers who have investigated use of reciprocal teaching have documented numerous studies demonstrating its effectiveness with varying grade levels and with English language learners (ELLs) (Klingner & Vaugh, 1996; Palincsar & David, 1991; Rosenshine & Meister, 1994).

EXPECTED LEARNER OUTCOME(S) ■ After completing the use of Reciprocal Teaching, learners are expected to have increased reading comprehension.

STEPS TO IMPLEMENTATION ■ The implementation of Reciprocal Teaching includes several steps that are designed to facilitate dialogue in the use of four comprehension strategies:

1. Select initial dialogue leader (i.e., teacher, other adult educator).
2. Students read the first paragraph or passage.
3. Dialogue leader generates questions focusing on four comprehension strategies.
4. Group engages in dialogue reflecting on the questions and drawing on information learned from the passage.
5. Dialogue leader summarizes passage after sufficient group discussion is completed.
6. Next paragraph or passage is read and new dialogue leader is selected.
7. Steps 1–5 are completed with each subsequent passage or paragraph.

▶ **Dialogue Questioning:** The educator who is directing the group of students begins a discussion about a passage read by asking questions that facilitate students' use of the four comprehension strategies. The leader poses questions and allows the students to respond, elaborate on, and comment on the questions and other group members' responses. Initially, scaffolding, think-aloud, and modeling are directed by the teacher; after students become familiar with the process, each group member takes a turn in the role of dialogue leader. The teacher adjusts the scaffolding to meet learner needs by applying supports such as prompts, modifications, praise, or feedback. After the group has completed the "dialogue" using the four comprehension strategies, the dialogue leader summarizes the paragraph discussed and may request predictions for the next passage to be read. The next dialogue leader is selected and the next passage is read. This process is continued until the entire passage has been read and discussed.

▶ **Comprehension Strategies:** One overall purpose of reciprocal teaching is to improve reading comprehension through use of four defined strategies as summarized here (Hoover et al., 2008):

Questioning—In this initial strategy, the dialogue leader asks questions about the passage to highlight the main idea (e.g., "What are the most important ideas in the passage?").

Clarifying—This is a self-monitoring strategy in which learners identify any unknown words, unfamiliar concepts, or aspects of the passage that they do not fully understand (e.g., "Which words or ideas are unknown to you?").

Summarizing—This strategy teaches learners the importance of being able to succinctly formulate a summary of the passage. The ability to develop a brief summary most likely indicates an understanding of the reading material (e.g., "In your own words give a summary of the passage").

Predicting—Students formulate guesses about what might happen next in the passage, using clues from the previous passage(s). Inability to generate somewhat accurate predictions indicates lack of understanding of the previously read passage(s) (e.g., "What do you think might happen next in the story?").

IMPLEMENTATION FIDELITY CHECK ■ Educators in each group observe student interactions and the process followed to implement reciprocal teaching. Fidelity involves ensuring that the students adhere to the steps to implementation and adequately address each of the four comprehension strategies.

INTERVENTION EFFECTIVENESS CHECKS ■ Reciprocal teaching is designed to improve reading comprehension.

▶ **Progress-Monitoring Data Collection Device(s):** Use ORF and MAZE passage or probe.

▶ **Frequency of Monitoring Data Collection:** Collect data every 10–12 school days.

▶ **Diagnostic Assessment:** Use individual reading comprehension tests (e.g., Test of Reading Comprehension, Gray Diagnostic Reading Tests).

▶ **Lack of Progress (Intervention Adjustments):** Reteach the four comprehension strategies. Allow a struggling student to be codialogue leader with either teacher or another student until the student understands the role better. Give the group of students a checklist to check off each step as it is completed. Scaffold the process by focusing on each individual comprehension strategy within a task and building up to application of all four strategies in the same reciprocal teaching reading task.

Intervention: *Classwide Peer Tutoring*

Primary Instructional Type	Primary Target Population	Primary Targeted Content Area(s)
___ Direct _X_ Cooperative ___ Independent	The primary target population is kindergarten students through twelfth graders.	The primary target content areas are reading, spelling, mathematics, and social studies.

INTERVENTION OVERVIEW ■ CWPT is a reciprocal peer tutoring intervention in which pairs (or dyads) of students work together as classroom teams. A game-type format is followed in which each dyad accumulates points for correct responses and the dyad that receives the most points wins the friendly competition. At the beginning of each week, the teacher selects one member of the pair to be the "tutor" and the other to be the "tutee." Two or more dyads are then placed on teams and, for that week, compete against each other. The dyads and team composition of pairs should change from week to week, increasing motivation and chances for each student eventually to be on the team with the most weekly points. Prior to beginning, CWPT students are trained in the role of tutor and tutee with specific emphasis on ways to ask questions, types of questions to ask, how to correct incorrect responses or mistakes, how to award points, and how to provide feedback. Teamwork, fair play, positive feedback, and role play are emphasized in CWPT. Dyad tutors and tutees assume their assigned roles for the week, and the dyad teams work together for the entire week. The CWPT process involves having the tutor ask questions and the tutee respond. Correct responses are awarded points and incorrect responses are corrected, as described in more detail in the following section.

INSTRUCTIONAL USAGE ■ CWPT is used when the primary educational goal is to activate prior knowledge, actively engage students in learning, and increase motivation to learn new content and material in the targeted content areas. Although it was originally developed for use with ELLs in the elementary grades (Greenwood, Arreaga-Mayer, Utley, Gavin, & Terry, 2001), the method is appropriate for use with students in grades K–12 and with students who have mild disabilities (Hoover et al., 2008).

RESEARCH-BASED EVIDENCE ■ CWPT is an EBI that is shown to affect reading comprehension and fluency (Greenwood et al., 2001). In addition, Arreaga-Mayer (1998) found that CWPT increased academic engagement and academic achievement (two primary goals of CWPT). CWPT is grounded in the eight constructs that are considered necessary to effectively teach students, including ELLs (Gersten & Jimenez, 1994): (a) respect for diversity, (b) scaffolding and use of cognitive strategies, (c) challenging curricula, (d) constructive feedback, (e) English as a Second Language (ESL) techniques and methods, (f) ongoing involvement, (g) cooperative learning, and (h) sufficient opportunities for success in learning.

EXPECTED LEARNER OUTCOME(S) ■ After completing the use of CWPT, learners are expected to have increased reading skills in the targeted content areas, increased active participation, ability to draw on the activation of prior knowledge, and increased motivation to learn.

STEPS TO IMPLEMENTATION ■ CWPT for reading is implemented adhering to four defined steps:

1. *Set-Up*—Careful thought and preparation on the part of the teacher is needed to set up the weekly instruction and structure for the dyads. This work includes selecting proper materials and assigning each student to a dyad. This initial step also includes the administration of a CBM probe designed to monitor progress in defined academic area(s) (e.g., oral reading fluency, knowledge of specific vocabulary at the beginning of the week).

2. *Training*—Teachers must spend sufficient time preparing the students for their roles as tutor or tutee and teaching them the procedures for asking questions, correcting mistakes, documenting points for correct responses, and providing feedback.

3. *Implementation*—At the beginning of each week, the teacher provides a brief minilesson on the reading material to be studied through CWPT. Initially, this lesson allows students the opportunity to draw on previous experiences and become prepared for the tutor–tutee interactions. After the minilesson, students are provided time to read silently the reading passage (e.g., 10 minutes). To begin the CWPT, the tutor presents a question (verbally or visually) to the tutee who, in turn, attempts to answer the question

(visually or orally). If the tutee is correct, two points are awarded; if the tutee is incorrect, the tutor provides the tutee the correct response. The tutee in turn must successfully write or say the correct response three times and receives one point after three successes occur. The types of questions asked by the tutor are "who, what, where, when, and why" questions and the training must include examples and practice in generating these types of questions, along with how to identify acceptable responses.

4. *Monitor*—Student progress is monitored in two ways: (a) informally as the teacher moves around the room listening to and observing the dyads in action, and (b) formally using the postassessment CBM probe monitoring progress identified in the Set-Up step. The informal monitoring allows the teacher to document the extent to which each student is actively engaged and demonstrating motivation, as well as visually determining the dyads' progress through collection of points. The pre–post CBM scores inform educators about the academic progress experienced by the learners through CWPT.

IMPLEMENTATION FIDELITY CHECK ■ CWPT has built-in fidelity checks in that the classroom teacher is moving around the room observing the different dyads in action, allowing the educator to determine the extent to which (a) tutors are asking proper questions, (b) tutees are responding to the questions, (c) tutors are providing correct responses when necessary, and (d) tutees eventually provide the correct response three times in a row.

INTERVENTION EFFECTIVENESS CHECKS ■ CWPT-Reading is designed to improve overall academic progress in reading fluency and comprehension.

▶ **Progress-Monitoring Data Collection Device(s):**   Use ORF and MAZE passage or probe.

▶ **Frequency of Monitoring Data Collection:**   Collect data every 10–12 school days.

▶ **Diagnostic Assessment:**   Use individual reading comprehension tests (e.g., Test of Early Reading Ability, Test of Silent Contextual Reading Fluency, Gray Oral Reading Test).

▶ **Lack of Progress (Intervention Adjustments):**   Reteach the four CWPT steps. Assist struggling student with selection of questions to ask in role of tutor. Give struggling tutee strategies for responding to tutor questions. Reinforce the training provided (in the second step) with periodic checks to ensure students are properly implementing CWPT. Strategically pair a struggling tutor or tutee with a strong student to facilitate initial successes.

Intervention: *Language Experience Approach*

Primary Instructional Type	Primary Target Population	Primary Targeted Content Area(s)
_X_ Direct ___ Cooperative ___ Independent	The primary target population is emergent readers (i.e., students showing reading readiness) in kindergarten and first grade, but this intervention is also appropriate for emergent readers in other grades, should their own vocabulary facilitate learning to read; the intervention is also effective with ELLs.	The primary target content area is reading.

INTERVENTION OVERVIEW ■ LEA (Allen, 1976) is a process to assist emergent readers to use their own language and vocabulary levels as the foundation for developing initial reading abilities. LEA is based on the learner's prior knowledge and interests (Hoover et al., 2008), so students use their own vocabulary and content in the material read. LEA increases motivation to learn to read and directly teaches the connections among speaking, writing, and reading. Although LEA is typically implemented with individual students, it may also be completed in small groups or with an entire class.

INSTRUCTIONAL USAGE ■ LEA is best used with emergent readers prior to formal reading. This group includes any emergent reader who benefits from use of his or her own vocabulary and reading interests as a beginning point in the initial reading process. LEA emphasizes a whole-to-part approach to acquiring reading in which students initially see the entire word or sentence and then break these down into their components. Therefore, LEA is a method that requires students to be able to learn via a whole-part process rather than a more phonetic approach of part-whole.

RESEARCH-BASED EVIDENCE ■ Success with the use of the LEA with emergent readers spans several decades and numerous research studies (Allen, 1976; Ashton-Warner, 1963; Sulzby & Barnhart, 1992). The LEA approach was found to be (a) effective at increasing word recognition, (b) more effective at the kindergarten level than first grade, and (c) most effective for the learner at the reading readiness level (Stahl & Miller, 2006). The LEA approach is effective for use with ELLs particularly due to its emphasis on a whole-part methodology (Haager & Klingner, 2005; Peregoy & Boyle, 2003).

EXPECTED LEARNER OUTCOME(S) ■ After completing the Language Experience Approach, emergent readers are more proficient with print awareness and word recognition, skills that establish the foundation for beginning formal reading.

STEPS TO IMPLEMENTATION ■ LEA requires educators to follow several steps, as described here, for an individual learner (Hoover et al., 2008):

1. Educator engages the learner in a discussion about personal experiences and asks him or her to select one topic of interest related to those experiences for further study.

2. Learner states a story about the selected topic and the teacher records the story verbatim using the student's vocabulary and modeling proper structure and punctuation.

3. Learner reads and rereads the story several times with teacher assistance as necessary.

4. Learner attempts to read the story independently several times and states the main idea of the story.

5. Learner copies or traces the words in the story, generates an illustration of the story, underlines or circles favorite words in the story, and rereads the written story several times.

6. Teacher prints words, phrases, and sentences from the story on word cards and sentence strips, and learner uses these words or phrases in various appropriate educational situations to assist with generalization of newly learned words and phrases.

7. Learner circles words or phrases from the story in other reading material.

8. Learner demonstrates word recognition (i.e., phonics) by identifying different types of words or phrases in the story as asked by the teacher (e.g., find all words that begin with the letter "b," find words that rhyme with "hat," find each time a certain phrase is used). Teacher also checks reading comprehension by using guiding questions.

After the process has been completed, the learner keeps the story in a binder and stores the word cards or strips in a file box. The student then generates another reading passage, following the same steps, building on the vocabulary and print awareness skills and improving comprehension. After the learner has developed basic emergent reading skills, he or she moves into formal beginning reading. An alternative to this process is to use a wordless picture book for a student who is in the initial stages of acquiring English as a second language. The student tells a story about the picture rather than relating personal experiences.

IMPLEMENTATION FIDELITY CHECK ■ Fidelity checks occur on a regular and consistent basis as the teacher engages the learner in the LEA process. A simple checklist may be developed and used to record implementation of each step within each LEA experience to document fidelity of implementation.

INTERVENTION EFFECTIVENESS CHECKS ▪ LEA is designed to improve readiness and early reading skills.

▶ **Progress-Monitoring Data Collection Device(s):**   Use ORF passage or probe and vocabulary lists.

▶ **Frequency of Monitoring Data Collection:**   Collect data every five school days.

▶ **Diagnostic Assessment:**   Use individual reading readiness and print awareness tests (e.g., Early Reading Assessment, Test of Word Reading Efficiency).

▶ **Lack of Progress (Intervention Adjustments):**   Refocus emphasis on student's most used vocabulary. Write words in sand or on raised paper for tactile tracing. Use flash cards more frequently to help struggling student's vocabulary recognition fluency. Have student type sentences on the computer in addition to writing on paper. Double the amount of time spent on each of the LEA Steps to Implementation.

Intervention: *Read Naturally Strategy*

Primary Instructional Type	Primary Target Population	Primary Targeted Content Area(s)
___ Direct ___ Cooperative X Independent	The primary target population is first graders through eighth graders.	The primary target content areas are reading fluency and phonics.

INTERVENTION OVERVIEW ▪ Read Naturally includes the individual application of specific steps and components that are designed to improve reading performance and that adhere to three interrelated core strategies: (a) teacher modeling, (b) repeated reading, and (c) progress monitoring (Read Naturally website). It uses audio recordings of a fluent reader, daily graphs of progress, and high-interest reading materials.

INSTRUCTIONAL USAGE ▪ The Read Naturally Strategy includes the above steps, along with specific materials, and is used with learners on an individual basis in grades 1–8 who require work in phonics and reading fluency and with students in grades 4–5 who need help in the area of vocabulary development. Phonemic awareness and comprehension are addressed in supplemental ways through the use of this strategy. The Read Naturally Strategy may be used to supplement existing programs (e.g., basal reading series) and as a complete program using program materials (e.g., Read Naturally Masters Edition, Software Edition, Progress Monitor, Benchmark Assessor). (See the Read Naturally website for complete descriptions and listing of materials.)

RESEARCH-BASED EVIDENCE ■ From the late 1990s through the 2008–09 school year, several studies were conducted on the effectiveness of the Read Naturally Strategy. In the various studies, the Strategy was used to supplement Basal Reading instruction and employed with Read Naturally reading materials and programs. Selected findings from the various studies show increased reading fluency, better reading comprehension, and more positive attitudes toward reading among students who receive supplemental Read Naturally Strategy support over those who do not, including special education students, learners with dyslexia, and ELLs (De La Colina, Parker, Hasbrouck, & Lara-Alecia, 2001; Hasbrouck, Ihnot, & Rigers, 1999; Read Naturally website).

EXPECTED LEARNER OUTCOME(S) ■ Learners are expected to increase skills and knowledge in reading fluency and phonics and to improve their vocabularies as they use the Read Naturally Strategy and associated materials. The program's website states "Our proven strategy, the combination of teacher modeling, repeated reading, and assessment and progress monitoring, benefits developing readers in many ways" (Read Naturally website).

STEPS TO IMPLEMENTATION ■ The Read Naturally website states procedures for using this strategy. Here are the steps that a student should follow to complete the *One-Minute Reader* process:

1. Select a story, read the title, look at the pictures, and consider what the story might be about, on the basis of this cursory overview.

2. Set the one-minute timer, read aloud for the minute, underline the words that you do not know, and mark the last word read when the timer goes off.

3. Subtract the number of words underlined from the number read and chart this result.

4. Insert the audio recording of the story you are reading into the CD player and read aloud along with the recording until you are able to read all the words (reading three times aloud is suggested).

5. Read the story alone several times. Read for one minute and mark the last word read; continue reading the rest of the story. Repeat this procedure several times until you can read without making any mistakes. Record the number of words read for each time on graphing chart. Most students will require 3–5 readings during this step.

6. Answer reading comprehension questions about the story and chart the number correct.

7. Read aloud while an adult records the number of incorrectly read words. Compare number of correctly read words with initial charting (Step 2) to record fluency progress. Also, review comprehension results with an adult.

The preceding steps are used for one of the Read Naturally program components and the reader is referred to the website for additional information or for steps to implement other program components.

IMPLEMENTATION FIDELITY CHECK ■ Educators who are monitoring the individual student's completion of the Read Naturally Strategy should observe the student to make certain that he or she completes all steps as designed, in the proper sequence, and completes all required documentation and charting.

INTERVENTION EFFECTIVENESS CHECKS ■ The Read Naturally Strategy is designed to improve phonics and reading fluency.

▶ **Progress-Monitoring Data Collection Device(s):** Use ORF passage or probe and running records.

▶ **Frequency of Monitoring Data Collection:** Collect data every five school days.

▶ **Diagnostic Assessment:** Use individual word recognition and fluency tests (e.g., Early Reading Assessment, Test of Early Reading Ability).

▶ **Lack of Progress (Intervention Adjustments):** Provide additional one-on-one instruction if student continues to struggle. Make certain Read Naturally reading material is similar to core reading instruction material. Improve *Implementation Step 4* by increasing the number of times the struggling student completes the read-along with the oral recording of the passage. Increase the number of times (e.g., 7–10) the struggling student reads passage silently to ensure consistent mastery of vocabulary and fluency.

Intervention: *Reading Response Journal*

Primary Instructional Type	Primary Target Population	Primary Targeted Content Area(s)
___ Direct ___ Cooperative _X_ Independent	The primary target population is any reader who is able to use writing to express feelings.	The primary target content areas are reading and reading motivation.

INTERVENTION OVERVIEW ■ Reading Response Journals (RRJs) provide students the opportunity to record their feelings about, reactions to, and impressions of the books they read (Hoover et al., 2008). The journaling occurs after each main reading activity; students record their thoughts and are then able to read what they have documented. This exercise, in turn, leads to additional comprehension of or reflection on the initially read material. Information recorded in the journals may also assist the learner to generate additional ideas when he or she is discussing the reading passage in small- or large-group settings.

INSTRUCTIONAL USAGE ■ RRJs are used with learners who possess basic writing skills or other means to record or express their thoughts, feelings, and impressions about a story immediately after an oral or silent reading activity. RRJs promote the "affective" side of reading rather than only emphasizing the plot or content of the story. Discussion of both the plot and effects of the plot on the reader provides a more complete examination of the reading material. This process provides success to all students who participate, as all affective aspects described by the learners are accepted during the discussions. An alternative to providing written responses for students who lack written expression skills is to have them draw an illustration or concept map to share their thoughts and feelings about the reading material.

RESEARCH-BASED EVIDENCE ■ The RRJ is based on reader response theory, which focuses on the role of the reader in the interpretation of reading material (Flood & Lapp, 1988). Response journals "are excellent tools to use when processing information after reading" (Chapman & King, 2003, p. 170).

EXPECTED LEARNER OUTCOME(S) ■ The primary intended outcomes in the use of RRJs are written (a) documentation of how the reading passage affects the learner, (b) impressions of the meaning of the story or passage, and (c) evidence of a deeper consideration of different aspects of the story that is unique to interpretations made by the learner.

STEPS TO IMPLEMENTATION ▪ RRJs are easy to guide and use with most learners. The following types of suggestions or instructions facilitate the effective use of RRJs:

1. Ensure that students know that the purpose of RRJs is to record their own impressions and feelings about the passage, rather than to "check" to make certain the story has been thoroughly read.

2. Suggest key types of items on which students may reflect:
   - Relate story ideas to own experiences.
   - Connect this reading with other previous readings.
   - Document passage components or statements that cause discomfort, happiness, confusion, etc.
   - Describe your personal reaction to a character's actions or specific story events.
   - Record specific quotes or statements that most affect you, provide meaning to you, or are relevant to you, and briefly explain why.

3. Allow learners the opportunity to share material recorded in the RRJs on a voluntary basis (i.e., do not force sharing).

4. Use information shared from the RRJs to stimulate additional discussion to assist learners to acquire deeper meanings for, impressions of, or analyses of the reading material.

IMPLEMENTATION FIDELITY CHECK ▪ As students share documented ideas and thoughts, teachers are able to determine the extent to which the RRJ is used properly (i.e., expression of feelings and thoughts, rather than summary of content read). In most situations, students will allow teachers to read their journals or students may read aloud to the educator what they have written, which also provides the opportunity for an implementation fidelity check. For those students who use an illustration or concept map to share feelings, asking them to provide a verbal narrative to the illustration provides additional confirmation that the RRJ is being used with fidelity.

INTERVENTION EFFECTIVENESS CHECKS ▪ RRJ is designed to improve reading motivation and comprehension.

▶ **Progress-Monitoring Data Collection Device(s):** Use MAZE passage and teacher-developed rubric recording the types of ideas shared.

▶ **Frequency of Monitoring Data Collection:** Collect data every 10 school days.

▶ **Diagnostic Assessment:** Use individual reading comprehension tests (e.g., Gray Silent Reading Tests, Test of Silent Contextual Reading Fluency).

▶ **Lack of Progress (Intervention Adjustments):** Provide struggling reader with targeted questions to focus learner's attention on specific impressions of the story. Provide struggling learner with opportunity to orally discuss the passage with a peer or teacher prior to recording impressions in journal. Allow struggling student to use concept map to express ideas and feelings.

Intervention: *Literature Response Group*

Primary Instructional Type	Primary Target Population	Primary Targeted Content Area(s)
___ Direct	The primary target population is any reader who is able to work in small reading groups.	The primary target content areas are reading comprehension and reading motivation.
_X_ Cooperative		
___ Independent		

INTERVENTION OVERVIEW ■ Literature Response Groups (LRGs) provide a structure for students to discuss what they are reading with peers in small-group settings (Peregoy & Boyle, 2001). Small groups of students (e.g., 3–6 individuals) who have read or had a story read to them meet on a regular basis to discuss the content, meanings, and impressions they have obtained from the reading material. A key feature of the LRGs is that learners are exposed to a variety of possible meanings and interpretations associated with the same reading material. This experience, in turn, supports development of critical thinking and flexibility in accepting various viewpoints.

INSTRUCTIONAL USAGE ■ LRGs are used with small groups of students to facilitate "meaningful dialogue with peers and to think deeply and critically about what they read (or had read to them)" (Hoover et al., 2008, p. 209). LRGs may be used with learners of all reading levels, as participation is based on individual reading, shared read-aloud, and/or having the entire passage read aloud.

RESEARCH-BASED EVIDENCE ■ The LRG method of instruction is based on successful ways of involving students in the reading comprehension process, including literature circles (Bos, 1991; Short & Klassen, 1993). LRG is a research-based method for facilitating active student participation in the discussion and interpretation of reading material, further developing reading motivation and comprehension (Hoover et al., 2008).

EXPECTED LEARNER OUTCOME(S) ■ Several expected outcomes result from the use of LRGs: (a) increased participation in reading discussions, (b) exposure to a variety of viewpoints and impressions about the same reading material, (c) interaction of learners with different reading levels about same reading material, and (d) more in-depth reading comprehension and motivation.

STEPS TO IMPLEMENTATION ■ The process for initiating and implementing LRGs may vary depending on student needs; however, several core elements are suggested for optimal use in the classroom:

▶ **Teacher Preparation:** Teacher models the following items:

Types of topics that students may address in their discussions (students may share, e.g., own responses or interpretations of a character's actions or positions)

Different viewpoints to illustrate that varying positions are acceptable and should be expected about the same reading material

Connections between events in a story to own personal experiences

▶ **Small-Group Process Development:** Students are prepared for work in the LRGs through the teacher modeling as described, along with guided practice in sharing personal impressions, interpretations, motivations, and reactions experienced when reading the material. Students also have practice with strategies for responding to others' viewpoints and interpretations.

▶ **Implementation:** Membership on each LRG is determined by the teacher. After their group has been formed, the students read the material or have the material read to them. To initiate discussion, one student begins a "dialogue" by sharing impressions of, thoughts about, or reactions to the material. Initially, this may be the result of a guided question that the teacher poses, assisting learners to become more familiar with the process. Other group members then share their impressions of, thoughts about, or reactions to the story and react to one another's shared information. The "dialogue" continues until the reading material has been addressed sufficiently, each group member has had an opportunity to share his or her own ideas, and each member has had the opportunity to respond to information shared by the other group members.

▶ **Conclusion:** Each LRG session may conclude in a variety of ways: (a) wrap up of key discussion points, (b) identification of the varying viewpoints expressed, (c) opportunity for group members to express one idea they acquired as a result of the discussions, (d) identification of types of topics to be considered during next LRG session, or (e) extension of the discussions to other learning experiences or tasks. Although the session may conclude in a variety of ways, the ending should provide an opportunity for group members to reflect on their learning and the value of these types of group discussions.

Students may record their impressions in a journal (i.e., RRJ) or a similar process for future reference. In addition, learners within LRGs may share their perceptions of the main ideas of the story (i.e., comprehension) and compare these views with their ideas acquired both before and after the discussions about the reading material.

IMPLEMENTATION FIDELITY CHECK ■ The fidelity of implementation of LRGs is determined by the teachers as they observe the groups in action, attending to the types of responses made and insights presented by different students. Teachers also ensure that all group members are involved in the dialogue to make certain each student has the opportunity to share his or her own impressions and ideas as well as react to those of others in the group.

INTERVENTION EFFECTIVENESS CHECKS ■ LRG is designed to improve reading motivation and comprehension.

▶ **Progress-Monitoring Data Collection Device(s):** Use MAZE passage or probe.

▶ **Frequency of Monitoring Data Collection:** Collect data every 10 school days.

▶ **Diagnostic Assessment:** Use individual reading comprehension tests (e.g., Test of Word Reading Efficiency, Test of Reading Comprehension).

▶ **Lack of Progress (Intervention Adjustments):** Provide struggling learner(s) with additional preparation and support for improved interactions within the small group. Adjust the composition of the small group to include students who can help struggling learners participate more effectively. Select reading passages that are of high interest to those who struggle. Assist struggling students to provide relevant impressions by asking them targeted questions about the passage.

Intervention: *Graphic Organizers*

Primary Instructional Type	Primary Target Population	Primary Targeted Content Area(s)
_X_ Direct ___ Cooperative ___ Independent	The primary target population is any reader who is able to use visuals to develop concepts.	The primary target content areas are reading vocabulary and concept development; however, this intervention is also appropriate to mathematics and other content areas.

INTERVENTION OVERVIEW ■ Preteaching key topics or concepts assists learners to succeed with upcoming reading passages. Various types of graphic organizers exist to organize key topics or concepts to assist learners to make connections among new vocabulary and concepts in reading material. These graphics include tree diagrams, semantic maps, concept maps, or word maps. The Graphic Organizers intervention provides learners with "a visual diagram of the relationship among key vocabulary terms that facilitates their understanding and retention of new words" (Hoover et al., 2008, p. 273). Initially, teachers provide direction in the development and use of one or more of the graphic organizers; then students work in small groups to develop their own. When they are used as a targeted intervention for preteaching in reading, Graphic Organizers assist learners to activate prior knowledge and put into context new vocabulary and concepts that are directly connected to new reading material. Use of graphic organizers provides learners opportunity to personalize their reading (Chapman & King, 2003).

INSTRUCTIONAL USAGE ■ Graphic Organizers are used with any reader to facilitate vocabulary and concept development associated with new material.

RESEARCH-BASED EVIDENCE ■ Use of a Graphic Organizer is a time-tested, research-based intervention to improve vocabulary and concept development, particularly for struggling readers. Graphic organizers have been found to be an effective intervention with all students, including those with disabilities and learners who are in the process of acquiring English as a second language (Bos & Anders, 1992; Kim, Vaughn, Wanzek, & Wei, 2004).

EXPECTED LEARNER OUTCOME(S) ■ Through use of Graphic Organizers, learners are expected to increase their vocabularies, acquire a better grasp of new concepts, activate their prior knowledge, and overall be able to interact with new reading material in more complete ways.

STEPS TO IMPLEMENTATION ■ Use of Graphic Organizers begins with a group-led teacher-directed activity to preteach key topics, vocabulary, or concepts associated with an upcoming reading passage, followed by student-led activities in small groups:

1. The teacher selects the type of organizer most appropriate to specific reading task (i.e., development of vocabulary, topic, or concept).
2. The selected skeleton diagram (e.g., tree, concept, word) is illustrated on a whiteboard or other visual medium and the key topic or concept to be pretaught is written on the diagram.
3. The teacher guides the group of students to complete the diagram with questions and discussion, having them brainstorm and share appropriate

words, phrases, or concepts that are associated with the key topic or concept being studied.

4. The teacher records the brainstorming efforts to complete the diagram and students discuss the completed diagram, sharing their impressions of the diagram and its importance to their development of the key topic or concept.

5. Students are divided into small groups who generate their own graphic organizers for subsequent key topics or concepts to be studied.

6. Students share their completed graphic organizers with others, explaining the documented content and discussing how the organizer assists them in the reading task.

IMPLEMENTATION FIDELITY CHECK ■ The fidelity of implementation in the use of one or more graphic organizers is easily monitored by the teacher during the teacher-directed steps and through observation during the student-led pairs or small groups. Application of the completed diagram ensures fidelity of implementation if students are able to apply the content of their diagrams to comprehend the reading passage and/or use the new vocabulary.

INTERVENTION EFFECTIVENESS CHECKS ■ Graphic Organizers are designed to improve reading vocabulary and concept development leading to increased comprehension.

▶ **Progress-Monitoring Data Collection Device(s):** Use MAZE passage or ORF probe.

▶ **Frequency of Monitoring Data Collection:** Collect data every 10 school days.

▶ **Diagnostic Assessment:** Use individual reading comprehension tests (e.g., Test of Reading Comprehension, Test of Silent Contextual Reading Fluency).

▶ **Lack of Progress (Intervention Adjustments):** Provide struggling reader with one-on-one teacher-directed instruction to demonstrate development of a graphic organizer. Allow struggling learner opportunity to develop several graphic organizers with a peer and then move back to small-group work. Provide struggling learner with a graphic organizer template that is partially completed and assist student to successfully complete remaining items. Debrief in a one-on-one teacher-directed situation to allow the struggling student to verbally articulate completed graphic organizer. Provide ongoing teacher support in the small-group situation by asking relevant questions to guide the student in completion of the graphic organizer.

Intervention: *Collaborative Strategic Reading*

Primary Instructional Type	Primary Target Population	Primary Targeted Content Area(s)
___ Direct <u>X</u> Cooperative ___ Independent	The primary target population is elementary and middle school students who possess adequate decoding skills yet have difficulties with reading comprehension, including ELLs.	The primary target content area is reading comprehension in content areas.

INTERVENTION OVERVIEW ■ Collaborative Strategic Reading (CSR) was originally developed to assist ELLs to become more successful with reading (Klingner & Vaughn, 1999). CSR is also an effective intervention for use with most learners to improve reading comprehension in the content areas, provided the learners possess adequate decoding skills. CSR blends cooperative learning and reciprocal teaching principles and practices to increase reading comprehension (Klingner, Vaughn, Dimino, Schumm, & Bryant, 2001). The goal of CSR is to provide learners with a more meaningful way to interact with grade-level content texts (e.g., science, social studies) in independent and cooperative ways. CSR assists students to construct meaning through discussion and interpretation of the content material that reflects their experiential backgrounds, self-concept, and background knowledge. CSR provides a meaningful alternative to the typical whole-class or teacher-directed approaches in teaching content material to elementary and middle school learners. CSR employs the student use of four reading strategies (Klingner et al., 2001):

Strategy 1: Preview—Students are provided eight minutes to preview the reading material by scanning the text and reviewing the charts, visuals, graphs, and main headings.

Strategy 2: Click and Clunk—When learners read the material, some of the content "clicks" with the learner and is easily comprehended. Other material "clunks"; the learner does not understand it and needs to spend additional time studying it. Students should document the material that "clunks" for later discussion.

Strategy 3: Get the Gist—To employ this strategy, students summarize the main ideas and synthesize different sections of material into key concepts or ideas. Learners may do this by writing a brief summary of the main points and/or sharing their summary verbally during class discussions of different sections of the reading material.

Strategy 4: Wrap Up—After completing Get the Gist, the students summarize the main points of the entire passage (i.e., combine ideas generated using Strategy 3) and create several questions about the text. The peers respond to the questions during small-group discussions. If the class has learning logs, students may also write what they learned through use of the four strategies within the CSR structure.

INSTRUCTIONAL USAGE ■ CSR is designed for use with small groups of learners to increase reading comprehension.

RESEARCH-BASED EVIDENCE ■ CSR improves reading comprehension compared with other reading approaches (Klingner, Vaughn, Arguelles, Hughes, & Ahwee, 2004). These authors also report that research supports the use of CSR to improve engagement of learners in the reading process. Overall, research spanning more than a decade of studies indicates that CSR improves (a) student engagement, (b) comprehension, (c) cooperative support, and (d) use of a variety of strategies (Klingner et al., 2004; Klingner & Vaughn, 2000; Klingner & Vaughn, 1996). In addition to improving reading comprehension, CSR was found to improve vocabulary and content learning, including progress with ELLs (Hoover et al., 2008).

EXPECTED LEARNER OUTCOME(S) ■ Elementary and middle school students who use CSR are expected to increase their comprehension of content material, such as science and social studies; become more engaged in the reading process; use a variety of reading strategies; and work cooperatively to acquire content knowledge and skills.

STEPS TO IMPLEMENTATION ■ Adhering to the following process assists students to successfully implement CSR:

1. *Strategy Training*—Students are taught each of the four strategies and provided opportunity to practice each. Generalization occurs in the reading of content material and is applied in the CSR small-group discussions.
2. *Identify Cooperative Roles*—Klingner et al. (2001) suggest that students be trained in the use of the following roles and assume these roles to implement student-led CSR:

   Leader: Leads the group in the CSR process and use of defined strategies and keeps the small group on task by suggesting when to move to the next reading passage.

   Clunk Expert: Guides the group members in the use of the strategies to clarify material requiring additional discussion (e.g., use of context clues) that group members recorded on their "clunk" cards.

Gist Expert: Guides the group in the "Get the Gist" activity, ensuring that the key ideas and topics for each section discussed include necessary information.

Announcer: Monitors the group interactions to ensure that each member participates and shares in the discussions (e.g., all members' "clunks" are addressed; one student speaks at a time).

Encourager: Provides encouragement to all members, commenting on positive group behaviors exhibited. Makes thoughtful comments and evaluates how well the group members worked together, providing suggestions for continued growth in creating and maintaining a positive group discussion environment.

3. *Group Interaction Skills Development*—The teacher trains students in effective group interaction skills, such as allowing each member to speak, listening while others speak, asking for feedback or clarification, taking turns sharing and speaking, valuing each member's contributions, and being supportive and understanding of others, especially those who have differing viewpoints.

4. *Beginning CSR Procedures*—The teacher reads aloud a passage to the whole class and models use of the four strategies until the students comprehend the material.

5. *Cooperative Group Discussions*—Students read subsequent passages and discuss the content, adhering to their assigned cooperative roles and employing the four reading strategies until the entire reading material has been read and discussed and all "clunk" aspects have been addressed.

IMPLEMENTATION FIDELITY CHECK ■ After students have engaged in their cooperative groups, the teacher is able to monitor each group to make certain student roles are implemented properly and content material is sufficiently addressed and discussed.

INTERVENTION EFFECTIVENESS CHECKS ■ CSR is designed to improve reading comprehension.

▶ **Progress-Monitoring Data Collection Device(s):** Use MAZE passage or ORF probe.

▶ **Frequency of Monitoring Data Collection:** Collect data every 30 school days.

▶ **Diagnostic Assessment:** Use individual reading comprehension tests (e.g., Test of Silent Contextual Reading Fluency, Test of Reading Comprehension).

▶ **Lack of Progress (Intervention Adjustments):** Make certain struggling learner possesses adequate decoding skills sufficient to be successful with CSR; if not, provide additional decoding supports. Prepare struggling learner for one of the cooperative roles and have student assume that role only until the role is mastered, at which time the student may move to another role. Pair struggling learner with a peer and have both assume the same CSR role until struggling student is able to successfully implement the role individually. Scaffold the training to target one of the four CSR strategies for the struggling learner, systematically building to subsequent strategies.

Intervention: *Peer-Assisted Learning Strategies–Reading*

Primary Instructional Type	Primary Target Population	Primary Targeted Content Area(s)
___ Direct _X_ Cooperative ___ Independent	The primary target population is K–12 students of any reading level.	The primary target content areas are reading comprehension and fluency.

INTERVENTION OVERVIEW ■ Peer-Assisted Learning Strategies (PALS) (Fuchs, Fuchs, & Burish, 2000) is a supplemental reading activity that pairs an average or high reader with a lower reader. Pairs of learners are selected on the basis of their reading fluency scores and pairs read together for approximately four weeks. The stronger readers support the efforts of those who are struggling through implementation of four reading strategies: (a) partner reading, (b) retelling, (c) paragraph shrinking, and (d) prediction relay. PALS reading materials are geared toward the lower reading level in each pair; implementation of PALS facilitates peer interactions and immediate corrective feedback (Haager & Klingner, 2005; McLeskley, Rosenberg, & Westling, 2010).

INSTRUCTIONAL USAGE ■ PALS is designed to be used in reading and mathematics instruction; reading is emphasized in this section. Specifically, PALS is used to improve reading comprehension and fluency for learners of all reading levels.

RESEARCH-BASED EVIDENCE ■ Within the general practice of peer tutoring, PALS has been shown to be highly effective in the area of reading. It is grounded in the CWPT intervention that was previously presented. Peer tutoring, including PALS, has been shown to improve academic and social outcomes for both the tutor and tutee in a variety of grade levels and content areas (McLeskley et al., 2010).

EXPECTED LEARNER OUTCOME(S) ■ Through use of PALS, learners are expected to increase their reading comprehension and reading fluency skill levels and to increase their active participation in the reading process.

STEPS TO IMPLEMENTATION ■ To implement PALS, follow these steps, as summarized in Hoover et al. (2008):

1. Gather oral reading fluency scores for all learners in the classroom and rank them in order from highest to lowest.

2. Divide the rank-ordered list in half and pair students together by pairing together the highest ranked students from each list (i.e., first highest in each half are paired; second highest in each half are paired; third highest are paired).

3. Select reading material for each pair that is geared toward the lower reader in each pair.

4. Provide training to all students in proper implementation of peer tutoring (e.g., questioning strategies, taking turns, supporting each other). Suggestions for preparing students to use peer-tutoring strategies may be found at kc.vanderbilt.edu/pals/.

5. Have pairs work together for a defined period of time (e.g., pairs may have three 30-minute sessions together per week for four weeks).

6. Pairs engage in partner reading adhering to the following steps for each of the four activities:

   Activity 1: Partner Reading—The stronger reader reads aloud for five minutes, and then the weaker reader reads the exact same material aloud for five minutes. If either reader misses a word, states the wrong word, or hesitates for more than four seconds, the other partner states Stop, you missed that word. Can you figure it out?" If after four seconds the reader is unable to state the word, the partner provides the word and then asks the partner to state the word. If the reader is successful, the partner states: "Good." The reader rereads the sentence and continues reading for the five-minute duration.

   Activity 2: Retelling—After the weaker reader has read for five minutes, the partner asks the reader to sequence the main ideas in the passage, retelling what has been read. The partner may ask questions such as "What did you learn first? Then what did you learn?" and the partners discuss until each main idea has been shared. This activity provides the weaker reader an opportunity to show his or her comprehension of the reading material.

   Activity 3: Paragraph Shrinking—During this activity, the stronger reader reads aloud for five minutes, stopping after each paragraph to summarize what was just read. Then the weaker reader reads aloud the NEXT passage for five minutes, stopping after each paragraph to summarize what was just read. The overall purpose of this activity is to summarize or "shrink" the reading material by identifying the main characters and reducing the main ideas to succinct statements of 10 or fewer words. The stronger reader may facilitate the dialogue with the weaker reader during this activity by asking targeted questions, such as "Who is the main person? What did this person do? What ideas did you learn from this paragraph?"

Activity 4: Prediction Relay—This activity uses half-page segments of text. After the partners have made predictions about what will happen in the story, the stronger reader reads first. The partners check and summarize their understanding of the passage, then the stronger reader continues with successive half-page segments for the five-minute duration. The weaker reader in turn completes the same process until the partners have completed the entire reading passage. During this activity, the pairs predict, read, check, and summarize:

> *Predict*—Prior to reading, predict what might happen in the passage.
>
> *Read*—Read a half-page section of a story.
>
> *Check*—Stop after reading the half-page to determine whether the prediction was accurate.
>
> *Summarize*—Provide a summary of the half-page passage.

PALS may be structured so that pairs of teams compete in a friendly competition and receive points for successful responses and supports provided to partners. Should teachers elect this option, they should clarify how points will be awarded for each pair during the peer-tutoring training sessions described. After the program has been implemented for the four-week period, teachers should perform a reading fluency check to monitor progress. (More frequent monitoring may be appropriate.)

IMPLEMENTATION OF FIDELITY CHECK ■ As students work together in their pairs the teacher observes student participation, notices supports that students provide to each other, and notes types of responses they give, along with the overall implementation of PALS the way it was designed to be implemented. Teacher observations may be followed by debriefing with students to ensure fidelity of implementation.

INTERVENTION EFFECTIVENESS CHECKS ■ PALS-Reading is designed to improve reading fluency and comprehension.

▶ **Progress-Monitoring Data Collection Device(s):** Use ORF and MAZE passage or probe.

▶ **Frequency of Monitoring Data Collection:** Collect data every 10–15 school days.

▶ **Diagnostic Assessment:** Use individual reading comprehension tests (e.g., Test of Early Reading Ability, Early Reading Assessment).

▶ **Lack of Progress (Intervention Adjustments):** Provide struggling learner additional training in the four PALS strategies and pair the student with the teacher to demonstrate use of each strategy. Pair struggling learner with a peer and have both assume the same PALS roles until the struggling student is able to successfully implement the role individually. Provide the struggling learner with some sample questions that are relevant to the reading passage to use as a guide for generating his or her own questions. Assist the struggling learner to master each of the four Activity Steps in sequential order. Forego the "competition" aspect to increase students' confidence and success.

Intervention: *Fernald Multisensory Reading Method*

Primary Instructional Type	Primary Target Population	Primary Targeted Content Area(s)
_X_ Direct	The primary target population is emergent readers.	The primary target content area is reading vocabulary.
___ Cooperative		
___ Independent		

INTERVENTION OVERVIEW ■ The Fernald Method, originally designed in the mid-twentieth century (Fernald, 1988), is a whole-word multisensory approach for developing vocabulary (particularly sight words) and related emergent reading skills (e.g., early use of words in a story, print awareness, left-right direction in reading) (Harris & Sipay, 1990). This method is for learners who exhibit significant problems acquiring vocabulary and beginning reading skills. It uses a multisensory approach in which students apply visual, auditory, and tactile methods to acquire new vocabulary.

INSTRUCTIONAL USAGE ■ The Fernald Multisensory Method is designed for use with emergent readers or other learners who benefit from the simultaneous use of visual, auditory, and tactile techniques to learning new vocabulary. The Fernald Method supports more traditional reading approaches for learners who are struggling with those reading methods (e.g., basal reading, linguistics approach) by providing a structure through which the use of touch, sight, and sound facilitate the acquisition of new vocabulary.

RESEARCH-BASED EVIDENCE ■ Multisensory approaches to developing reading vocabulary, such as the Fernald Method, have been found to be effective with students who have more significant needs and who repeatedly do not respond to other methods, resulting in repeated failures with emergent reading skills and vocabulary development (Harris & Sipay, 1990). In addition, the Fernald Method has been found to provide struggling learners with the systematic study of words, necessary repetition, reinforcement of left-to-right direction in reading, and immediate feedback that they need to achieve success (Harris & Sipay, 1990). When it is used after the student has been unsuccessful with other forms of reading instruction, the Fernald Method may provide the necessary structure, support, and learning style to assist struggling students with supplemental vocabulary development to begin the early reading process.

EXPECTED LEARNER OUTCOME(S) ■ Students who use the Fernald Multisensory Approach are expected to increase their vocabulary development and the application of those words in reading contexts.

STEPS TO IMPLEMENTATION ■ Implementation of the Fernald Method is completed through four steps or stages (Mercer, Mercer, & Pullen, 2011):

Stage 1: Tactile Word Acquisition—The student selects a word to be learned and the teacher writes the word in larger letters, which the student then traces with his or her finger while saying the word out loud. The task of tracing and saying the word generates the multisensory aspects of this method as the student sees the word (visual), traces the word (tactile), and says the word aloud (auditory). After the student has been successful tracing and saying the word, he or she writes it. If the student makes an error in any of these tasks, the process is started over; success requires that the student correctly writes the entire word. After it has been written, the word is kept in a word file box for future use. The student's words are in turn used to create sentences, which the student also writes. The sentences are then used to create stories. Stage 1 of the Fernald Method assists students to learn new words of their choosing by (a) demonstrating the new vocabulary tactilely, visually, and auditorily; (b) writing each new word; (c) using the new words to create sentences; and (d) using the sentences to create written stories. Successful repetitions in the application of Stage 1 provide students the foundation to begin to acquire new vocabulary without tracing.

Stage 2: Building Vocabulary—During this stage, the learner continues to build vocabulary without tracing the words. The student continues to select words to be learned and the teacher writes the words. However, during this stage the student looks at the word (visual), says the word (auditory), and writes the word, putting it in the word file box. The student continues to create new sentences and written stories with the new words. When the student no longer requires the teacher to write the word in order to learn new vocabulary, Stage 2 is completed.

Stage 3: Beginning Reading—During this stage, the student is able to learn new vocabulary by looking at printed words in the text (i.e., seeing, saying, and writing the new word). The teacher no longer needs to write the word for the student. As the student is able to learn new words within existing print, he or she begins reading books. The student reads aloud and the teacher is able to determine the extent to which new vocabulary is acquired.

Stage 4: Expanded Reading Skills—After the learner has become more proficient at reading beginning stories, he or she will be better able to acquire new vocabulary, as the student will be able to recognize new words on the basis of their similarities to already acquired vocabulary. This experience in turn improves fluency, comprehension, and vocabulary development.

Use of the Fernald Method in reading provides struggling learners with a highly structured, multisensory approach for initially developing reading vocabulary and basic written language skills, leading to the development of emergent and early reading abilities. This whole-word approach uses tactile, auditory, and visual tasks and allows newly acquired vocabulary to be put into a reading/writing context immediately for added authenticity and relevance.

IMPLEMENTATION FIDELITY CHECK ■ The teacher is directly involved with the process as the student engages in each of the four stages. The teacher performs fidelity of implementation checks by reflecting on the process on a regular and consistent basis.

INTERVENTION EFFECTIVENESS CHECKS ■ Fernald is designed to improve early reading vocabulary.

▶ **Progress-Monitoring Data Collection Device(s):** Use ORF passage or probe and vocabulary lists.

▶ **Frequency of Monitoring Data Collection:** Collect data every five school days.

▶ **Diagnostic Assessment:** Use individual reading vocabulary tests (e.g., Early Reading Assessment, Test of Early Reading Ability, Decoding Skills Test).

▶ **Lack of Progress (Intervention Adjustments):** Refocus emphasis on student's most used vocabulary. Rewrite words in sand or on raised paper for tactile tracing. Use flash cards more frequently to help struggling student's vocabulary recognition fluency. Have student type sentences on the computer in addition to writing on paper. Double the amount of time spent on each of the Fernald Steps to Implementation.

Intervention: *Self-Questioning*

Primary Instructional Type	Primary Target Population	Primary Targeted Content Area(s)
___ Direct ___ Cooperative _X_ Independent	The primary target population is any reader in grades K–12.	The primary target content area is reading comprehension.

INTERVENTION OVERVIEW ■ Self-Questioning in reading assists learners to activate prior knowledge, generate explanations about the reading material, and monitor their comprehension. "Self-questioning stimulates students' use of prior knowledge to make facts and difficult text more comprehensible and memorable" (Reutzel, Camperell, & Smith, 2002, p. 327). Students also maintain active engagement in the process of reading through self-questioning. For example, the question prompts the student to explore necessary supports or additional reading to develop an acceptable response. This process requires the student to draw on prior knowledge and experiences connected to the reading material, thereby increasing his or her chances of success with comprehending the reading passage.

INSTRUCTION USAGE ■ Self-questioning may be used with any reader to further develop comprehension by activating prior knowledge or experiences. This intervention is especially valuable for students who require a structure and process to become more actively engaged in reading tasks.

RESEARCH-BASED EVIDENCE ■ Effective use of self-questioning in reading has been shown to be a learning quality that is possessed by more effective readers over those with less proficient reading comprehension (Cote & Goldman, 1999; Reutzel et al., 2002).

EXPECTED LEARNER OUTCOME(S) ■ Self-questioning has several expected outcomes: (a) increased active engagement in the reading process, (b) use of a prompt to initiate additional supports for reading, (c) use of prior knowledge to advance reading comprehension of new or unfamiliar material, and (d) increased reading comprehension.

STEPS TO IMPLEMENTATION ■ Self-questioning (Wong & Jones, 1982) involves five steps:

1. Know the reason for studying the passage.
2. Identify and underline main idea(s).
3. Generate a good question about the main idea(s) underlined.

4. Read more closely to answer your question(s).

5. Review answer to determine how response provides more information about main idea(s).

IMPLEMENTATION FIDELITY CHECK ■ Implementation fidelity of self-questioning focuses primarily on the extent to which the learner is generating questions that are appropriate to the reading material. The use of self-questioning is an independent learner activity and therefore requires the teacher periodically to discuss or debrief with the students the types of questions generated, and more importantly, to discuss how these questions led to improved comprehension (e.g., pre–post checks).

INTERVENTION EFFECTIVENESS CHECKS ■ Self-Questioning is designed to improve reading comprehension.

▶ **Progress-Monitoring Data Collection Device(s):** Use MAZE passage or probe.

▶ **Frequency of Monitoring Data Collection:** Collect data every 10 school days.

▶ **Diagnostic Assessment:** Use individual reading comprehension tests (e.g., Test of Silent Contextual Reading Fluency, Test of Reading Comprehension).

▶ **Lack of Progress (Intervention Adjustments):** Provide struggling reader with one-on-one teacher-directed instruction to demonstrate development of relevant self-questions. Allow struggling learner opportunity to develop several questions with a peer and then move back to independent reading. Provide struggling learner with a self-questioning template to help student activate prior knowledge. Debrief in a one-on-one teacher-directed situation to allow the struggling student to verbally articulate the rationale for selected self-questions. Provide ongoing teacher support in the independent self-questioning situation by asking relevant questions to guide the student in posing and responding to questions.

Intervention: *Reader's Theater*

Primary Instructional Type	Primary Target Population	Primary Targeted Content Area(s)
___ Direct _X_ Cooperative ___ Independent	The primary target population is any reader in the lower elementary grades.	The primary target content areas are reading comprehension and fluency.

INTERVENTION OVERVIEW ■ Reader's Theater is an intervention that stresses repeated and guided oral reading. This intervention supports the reading and rereading of scripts with emotion, expression, and feelings (Richard-Amato, 1996). Reader's Theater is interactive and improves learners' comprehension and fluency through repeated readings of the same script (Trainin & Andrzejczak, 2006). In addition, the repetition facilitates learners' vocabulary development and comprehension without having them do conscious memorization (Richard-Amato, 1996).

INSTRUCTIONAL USAGE ■ Reader's Theater may be used with all learners. Its use has been shown to be highly effective with students who require repeated reading to improve comprehension and fluency.

RESEARCH-BASED EVIDENCE ■ Researchers have identified that Reader's Theater promotes motivation, helps students see a meaningful context for rereading material, and encourages active engagement. Rasinski and Hoffman (2003) suggest the importance of Reader's Theater as a repeated reading intervention. Trainin and Andrzejczak (2006) found through their series of research studies that Reader's Theater was effective at improving both reading comprehension and reading fluency.

EXPECTED LEARNER OUTCOME(S) ■ Expected learner outcomes in the use of Reader's Theater include increased motivation, active engagement, reading fluency, and comprehension.

STEPS TO IMPLEMENTATION ■ To successfully implement Reader's Theater, select stories that are brief; that contain an obvious beginning, middle, and end; and that contain several characters so that a group of learners may cooperatively participate. The following steps to implement each Reader's Theater script and production were developed from discussions found in Peregoy and Boyle (2001):

1. Assist students to select appropriate and engaging reading material. Stories may be downloaded from various websites (e.g., www.teachingheart. net/readerstheater.htm).
2. Provide each student a copy of the script.
3. Coach students in the use of proper diction, dramatization, expression, and gestures.
4. Establish a daily routine for reading the scripts.
5. Implement Reader's Theater for a defined time period (e.g., 20 minutes a day for 12 weeks).
6. Guide students to read their parts in the script with expression (material is not memorized).

7. Have students share their analysis and comprehension of the story.

8. Have students develop the presentation of the story for delivery to others in the class, grade, or school.

9. Have a "cast" of students rehearse the script and production until it is ready for presentation to others, then deliver the production to others.

10. After the performance, measure student fluency levels (through, e.g., AIMSweb) and develop a simple CBM probe to measure comprehension of the specific scripted material.

IMPLEMENTATION FIDELITY CHECK ■ Reader's Theater is primarily completed cooperatively as students discuss and encourage each other in the reading of the script and developing the production. Fidelity of implementation is determined through the teacher's observations of student participation and delivery of the production.

INTERVENTION EFFECTIVENESS CHECKS ■ Reader's Theater is designed to improve reading fluency and comprehension.

▶ **Progress-Monitoring Data Collection Device(s):** Use ORF and MAZE passage or probe.

▶ **Frequency of Monitoring Data Collection:** Collect data every 10 school days and after production is complete.

▶ **Diagnostic Assessment:** Use individual reading comprehension tests (e.g., Test of Reading Comprehension, Gray Diagnostic Reading Tests).

▶ **Lack of Progress (Intervention Adjustments):** Provide struggling learner a role that allows for initial success with less oral reading and increase reading as learner demonstrates success. Ensure that the topic of the passage read aloud is of high interest to struggling reader. Review with the struggling learner the script prior to its use with the group to ensure that the learner knows all words. Preread the script aloud with the struggling student through one-on-one teacher-directed instruction or in a paired peer situation.

Intervention: *Reading Recovery*

Primary Instructional Type	Primary Target Population	Primary Targeted Content Area(s)
_X_ Direct ___ Cooperative ___ Independent	The primary target population is first-grade high-risk readers.	The primary target content areas are emergent and early reading skills (i.e., letter-sound associations and vocabulary development).

INTERVENTION OVERVIEW ■ Reading Recovery (Clay, 1993) is an intensive intervention program with specific strategies and steps designed to supplement general class Tier 1 reading curricula for learners in first grade who are struggling to develop beginning reading skills. The teacher implements the intervention one-on-one with the student for approximately 30 minutes each day. This intervention emphasizes vocabulary development and letter–sound associations by having the student complete a series of defined steps stressing repetition and familiar phonetically regular words.

INSTRUCTIONAL USAGE ■ Reading Recovery helps beginning and low-achieving first-grade students develop phonics skills within relevant and meaningful contexts.

RESEARCH-BASED EVIDENCE ■ Mercer et al. (2011, p. 284), citing Pinnell (1990), wrote that research on the effects of Reading Recovery "indicates that it has both immediate and long-term effects in helping low-achieving students to read." D'Agostino and Murphy (2005) found that Reading Recovery is effective in helping low-achieving students learn to read. In addition, an Institute of Education Sciences (2008) What Works Clearinghouse report on the effectiveness of Reading Recovery stated that the method has demonstrated success in developing general reading achievement and has potential positive effects on reading comprehension and fluency.

EXPECTED LEARNER OUTCOME(S) ■ Learners who are taught using the Reading Recovery intervention are expected to increase their general reading ability with improved comprehension and fluency.

STEPS TO IMPLEMENTATION ■ Reading Recovery involves several steps, implemented in 30-minute reading sessions (Clay, 1985; Mercer et al., 2011):

1. Student rereads two easy books (selected from a list of 700 books).
2. Teacher completes a running record (10-minute oral reading in which the teacher records reading errors and reading strategies used by the student on the selected books.
3. Student works with individual letters by manipulating them on a magnetic board (e.g., identifying letters, sounding out letters, finding letters within words).
4. Student dictates a sentence and works with the teacher to spell and write words correctly using appropriate strategies.
5. Student writes the sentence, correctly spelling all words, and reads the written sentence.
6. Teacher writes the sentence on a sentence strip and makes it into cut strips.
7. Student is asked to recreate the sentence using cut strips.

8. Student prepares to read an unfamiliar book and repeats the preceding steps.

9. Teacher keeps periodic running records and charts the results to illustrate vocabulary development and letter–sound association progress.

This process is completed for 20 weeks and is discontinued only when the student achieves grade-level reading. Reading Recovery includes a 30-hour training prior to beginning the intervention and a year-long training course that meets for 2.5 hours per week during the school year. This intervention requires more concentrated training than the other interventions described in this chapter. The reader is referred to the Reading Recovery website for additional information (readingrecovery.org/).

IMPLEMENTATION FIDELITY CHECK ■ Reading Recovery is a highly structured and scripted intervention requiring extensive training and specific uses of materials with individual students. It is important for the teacher to adhere to stated implementation process. The teacher should periodically run through a simple checklist to make certain that this intervention is being implemented as it was designed.

INTERVENTION EFFECTIVENESS CHECKS ■ Reading Recovery is designed to improve readiness and early reading skills.

▶ **Progress-Monitoring Data Collection Device(s):** Use ORF passage or probe and running records.

▶ **Frequency of Monitoring Data Collection:** Collect data every five school days.

▶ **Diagnostic Assessment:** Use individual reading readiness and print awareness tests (e.g., Early Reading Assessment, Test of Word Reading Efficiency).

▶ **Lack of Progress (Intervention Adjustments):** Extend the amount of time allotted to each of the required steps. Make certain to select books from the required list that are of high interest to the struggling learner. Allow student to use computer to write sentences periodically to improve success.

Intervention: *Incremental Rehearsal*

Primary Instructional Type	Primary Target Population	Primary Targeted Content Area(s)
_X_ Direct ___ Cooperative ___ Independent	The primary target population is struggling readers in the elementary grades.	The primary target content areas are vocabulary development and fluency.

INTERVENTION OVERVIEW ■ Incremental Rehearsal (Tucker, 1989) is an intervention for teaching high-frequency and other vocabulary words to struggling readers. This intervention is highly structured and incorporates "systematic procedures that facilitate mastery, build fluency, and lead to retention of skills for struggling readers" (Joseph, 2006, p. 803). The theoretical foundation for use of Incremental Rehearsal is the premise that students are more successful with academic tasks that include both known material and unknown material (Skinner, 2002). The development of new vocabulary through this intervention includes the simultaneous study of both known and unknown words using flash cards, reflecting a specified known/unknown ratio (90% known to 10% unknown). The student systematically states the unknown words, then the known words, until the unknown words become known words.

INSTRUCTIONAL USAGE ■ Incremental Rehearsal is used with learners who struggle with acquiring new vocabulary, especially high-frequency words (e.g., sight words) that are found in grade-level reading material.

RESEARCH-BASED EVIDENCE ■ Research on Incremental Rehearsal shows that students retain most of the new vocabulary words within two or three days of using this intervention. They learn words with both regular and irregular spelling patterns, and some research findings suggest that they are able to generalize the newly acquired words into oral reading passages (Joseph, 2006). Incremental Rehearsal also increases vocabulary and reading fluency (MacQuarrie, Tucker, Burns, & Hartman, 2002; Roberts & Shapiro, 1996).

EXPECTED LEARNER OUTCOME(S) ■ Through use of Incremental Rehearsal, learners are expected to expand their vocabulary, recognize newly acquired words in reading passages, and increase their motivation to learn.

STEPS TO IMPLEMENTATION ■ The implementation of Incremental Rehearsal includes adherence to several drill and practice steps using flash cards (Joseph, 2006):

1. Identify 9 known words and 10 unknown words and write all 19 words on individual flash cards.

   FIRST WORD: Show the student the first UNKNOWN word and say it while the student looks at the word, then have the student say the word. Show the student the first KNOWN word and ask the student to say the word. Present again the first UNKNOWN word and have the student say the word, then have the student say the first and second KNOWN words. Present again the first UNKNOWN word and have the student say the word, then have the student say the first, second, and third KNOWN words. Repeat this process, going through all nine KNOWN words. An

UNKNOWN word becomes a KNOWN word when the student automatically says the word correctly at least twice in a row. After the first UNKNOWN word has become a KNOWN word, replace it with the ninth KNOWN word (i.e., the newly acquired word becomes the new ninth KNOWN word). Begin the process again using the second UNKNOWN word.

SECOND WORD: Show the student the second UNKNOWN word and say it while the student looks at the word, then have the student say the word. Show the student the first KNOWN word and ask the student to say the word. Present again the second UNKNOWN word and have the student say the word, then have the student say the first and second KNOWN words. Present again the second UNKNOWN word and have the student say the word, then have the student say the first, second, and third KNOWN words. Repeat this process, going through all nine KNOWN words. After the student has learned the second UNKNOWN word, replace it as the eighth KNOWN word (i.e., the second newly acquired word becomes the new eighth KNOWN word). Repeat the process using the third UNKNOWN word.

2. Complete these procedures for each of the 10 unknown words. Say the unknown word and then say one known word, say the unknown word and then say the first two known words, and repeat until all nine known words have been stated in conjunction with each unknown word. Repeat this process until all 10 unknown words become known words. Then the teacher should posttest the learner on all 10 initially unknown words without using the known words to determine mastery. Continue the use of Incremental Rehearsal with a new set of 10 unknown words coupled with 9 known words. Although in this scenario the teacher is working with the student, a pair of students could complete the process by themselves with teacher monitoring.

IMPLEMENTATION FIDELITY CHECK ■ Implementation fidelity in the use of Incremental Rehearsal occurs if all steps are followed as designed. This process ensures that overlearning occurs and facilitates mastery of newly acquired vocabulary. Teachers should be certain that the sequence for saying the unknown and known words is properly followed until all nine unknown words have been addressed and mastered.

INTERVENTION EFFECTIVENESS CHECKS ■ Incremental Rehearsal is designed to improve reading vocabulary and fluency.

▶ **Progress-Monitoring Data Collection Device(s):** Use ORF passage or probe and vocabulary lists.

▶ **Frequency of Monitoring Data Collection:** Collect data every five school days.

▶ **Diagnostic Assessment:** Use individual reading vocabulary tests (e.g., Test of Word Reading Efficiency, Test of Silent Contextual Reading Fluency).

▶ **Lack of Progress (Intervention Adjustments):** Refocus emphasis on most widely used high-frequency vocabulary. Use flash cards more frequently to help struggling student's vocabulary recognition fluency. Provide struggling student guidance in identifying words in actual reading passages and books to help improve generalization.

Research-Based Comprehensive Reading Programs

A key strength in using the preceding EBIs is that they may be used along with or supplemental to a variety of comprehensive Tier 1 core reading curricula that are already in use in the classroom. With the exception of Read Naturally and Reading Recovery, each of the reading interventions described requires little or no purchasing of separate materials, which makes them highly usable and functional for classrooms where some learners' reading needs require additional supports.

Numerous comprehensive **research-based reading programs** also exist for use to implement evidence-based practice with struggling learners. These programs are designed for use with learners who require extensive supplemental teaching (i.e., Tier 2) or intensive instruction (i.e., Tier 3). Several of these research-based reading programs are summarized in Table 4.3. These programs are comprehensive, as they include necessary materials, activities, supports, enrichment, and core instruction in the key reading instructional areas (e.g., phonics, comprehension, fluency, vocabulary). Because these programs may be expensive and therefore may not be available in different schools, information about them is provided in order to share the key aspects of the programs, and the reader is referred to each program's citation for additional information.

Teacher and Student Strategies for Differentiated Reading Instruction

In addition to comprehensive RBCs and the structured EBIs for reading, there are numerous **teaching and student strategies** to ensure implementation of a differentiated classroom. A variety of teaching and behavior management techniques and study strategies were presented in Chapter 2, including many strategies that are specific to differentiating reading instruction to prevent learner

TABLE 4.3 Reading Research-Based Comprehensive Programs for Struggling Learners

Program	Brief Description
Reading Mastery (Engelmann & Bruner, 2002)	Highly structured, fast-paced reading program for students in grades K–6. This direct instruction approach provides students development in phonics and comprehension skills through a teacher-scripted program.
Corrective Reading Program (Englemann, Johnson, & Carnine, 1999)	Corrective Reading (similar to Reading Mastery) is geared toward older students and adults. Decoding and comprehension are emphasized for learners who are in fourth grade and above.
Horizons: Learning to Read (Engelmann, Engelmann, & Davis, 1998)	Highly structured and scripted program integrating spelling and reading for first- and second-grade low readers or nonreaders. The program focuses on letter combinations, rhyming, silent letters, and phonetically decodable and irregular words. A program for students in third grade and above is also available.
Wilson Reading System (wilsonlanguage. com)	Highly structured reading program for learners in second grade through adult. Program emphasizes decoding, encoding, oral reading fluency, vocabulary, and comprehension through multisensory and interactive strategies using highly controlled and decodable texts.
Edmark Reading Program (Edmark, 1972)	For use with low-achieving students, including those with mild disabilities, who read below the third-grade reading level. It is a highly repetitive program emphasizing emergent and early reading skills (e.g., sight words, capital letters, punctuation, word endings). The recently revised Edmark (available through Pro-Ed Publishers) is delivered through a series of modules and is especially effective at teaching sight word vocabulary.
Reading Milestones (Quigley, McAnally, King, & Rose, 2001)	This program is appropriate for use with elementary school students with hearing impairments, language delays, and learning disabilities. The program emphasizes high frequency words and regular spelling patterns using word phases, picture clues, and controlled vocabulary and syntax. Reading Milestones prepares students for reading at the fourth- and fifth-grade levels.
Reading Recovery (Clay, 1993)	Intensive intervention program for learners in first grade who are struggling to develop beginning reading skills.
Read Naturally (Read Naturally Website)	Program for learners in grades 1–8 who require work in phonics and reading fluency and for students in grades 4–5 who need help in the area of vocabulary development.
Scholastic READ 180 (Scholastic Website)	Intensive and motivating reading program for general and special education upper elementary and secondary students who exhibit two or more years of below-grade-level reading proficiency.
Scholastic System 44 (Scholastic Website)	Foundational reading program for students with significant reading needs in grades 3–12, providing high-interest reading materials and motivating adaptive technology.
SpellRead (PCI Education Website)	Multisensory program for struggling readers in grades 2 and above, including special education students and English language learners, designed to improve phonological skill development.

TABLE 4.4 Teacher and Student Strategies for Differentiating Reading Instruction*

Reading Strategy	Focus Area(s)	Teacher	Student
FIST	Comprehension		X
KWL	Comprehension		X
Panorama	Comprehension		X
PARS	Comprehension		X
PQ4R	Comprehension		X
RAP	Comprehension		X
ReQuest	Comprehension		X
RIDER	Mental Imagery		X
SQ3R	Comprehension		X
Contingency Contract	General Reading	X	
Planned Movement	Multiple Reading Tasks	X	
Simply Reading Level	Vocabulary; Comprehension	X	
Self-Monitoring	On-Task Reading Behaviors		X
Prompting	Vocabulary; Fluency	X	
Shortened Assignments	Oral Reading; Reviews	X	

*Each strategy is identified as being primarily directed either by the teacher or by the student.

needs from becoming more significant. Unlike those more highly structured EBIs, the teacher and student strategies in this chapter are often simple techniques requiring little prior training that are easily incorporated into (a) any classroom structure, (b) Tier 1 core curriculum, and (c) Tier 2 supplemental supports. Table 4.4 provides a list of the reading-based teacher and student strategies that were previously presented in Tables 2.1 and 2.2 to remind the reader of appropriate reading-based differentiations.

As shown, several easy-to-use teacher and student strategies exist to improve reading, specifically reading comprehension. Use of these teacher and student strategies may prevent needs from becoming more significant, reducing the need for more resource-intensive Tier 2 instruction. Should Tier 2 instruction be warranted, these strategies may be continued to further differentiate instruction for struggling readers.

CONCLUSION

The identification of learning needs through the use of achievement screening and progress monitoring is an initial first step in helping all learners progress in school. After educators have identified learners' needs, their next challenge is to (a) ensure that a differentiated classroom exists in which teachers and students employ a variety of simple-to-implement differentiation strategies as well as selected EBIs, (b) make correct decisions concerning the implementation of Tier 2 instruction requiring proper selection of evidence-based reading interventions, or (c) select use of a more comprehensive RBC to meet more significant needs (i.e., Tier 3). The key to these three tasks is sufficient understanding of why and how to use selected differentiated strategies, EBIs, and/or RBCs. Through careful study of the reading strategies, curricula, and interventions described in this chapter, educators become more informed and are able to make more effective reading instructional adjustments associated with screening or progress monitoring of data-based decisions associated with Tiers 1, 2, and 3 instruction.

CHAPTER 5

Evidence-Based Writing Practices

▶ ## Chapter Overview

THE PROCESS OF TEACHING writing to any learner reflects an integrated set of skills that requires effective uses of higher order thinking abilities, vocabulary, and sentence structure. A writer must also have knowledge of word meanings and the ability to produce readable work in order to transmit his or her ideas, thoughts, and intentions in a written format. A variety of writing interventions exist to teach all students, including struggling writers, to be more proficient with written expression. This chapter provides coverage of key writing interventions, strategies, and programs to meet multi-tiered writing needs.

Key Terms

- ▶ Learning strategies
- ▶ Self-regulated learning
- ▶ Writing process

Writing Content Areas and Multi-Tiered Instructional Interventions

Written Expression

Select a written expression intervention that targets the assessed content
area in which the learner demonstrates inadequate writing progress.

Writing Intervention	Writing Strategies	Revising Material	Prewriting
Self-Regulation Strategy Development Model	X		
Focus Correction Areas		X	
Report Writing Strategy			X
Compare-Diagnose-Operate Strategy		X	
Peer Revising Strategy		X	
Evaluation Strategy: Writing	X		
Active Processing: Writing	X		X

INTRODUCTION

Students who struggle with writing tasks may exhibit a variety of writing needs. In order for them to improve their written expression, they must master several instructional components that are described in this chapter. However, prior to addressing the key individual elements associated with effective written expression, we will discuss the overall **writing process**, an understanding of which is necessary in order to ensure proper interpretation of writing screening and progress-monitoring data scores.

Writing as a Process

Fundamental to teaching students how to write within a multi-tiered model is the implementation with fidelity of a structured writing process model, several of which have been developed and frequently emphasized in writing literature and programs (Echevarria & Graves, 2007; Graham, MacArthur, & Fitzgerald, 2007; Graves, 2008; Mercer, Mercer, & Pullen, 2011; Tompkins, 2008). These different models include a variety of essential writing components that are necessary to implement an effective writing process.

FIGURE 5.1   Essential Components to Teaching Writing

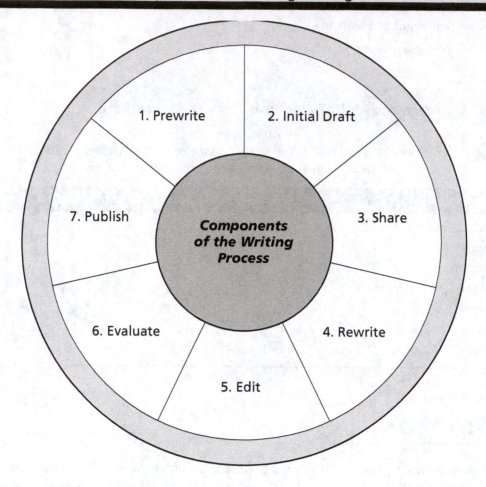

1. Prewrite
2. Initial Draft
7. Publish
Components of the Writing Process
3. Share
6. Evaluate
4. Rewrite
5. Edit

Figure 5.1 illustrates one writing process model that was developed from discussions in the sources mentioned. The model includes elements that are considered essential in teaching writing to students and that are discussed in greater detail following the figure.

As shown, the seven-step process begins with prewriting activities, progresses to writing and editing tasks, and culminates with publishing the written work. Each of the steps requires direct instruction. When screening and progress-monitoring data scores indicate that a writer is struggling, the teacher should confirm that this instruction process is being implemented with fidelity in Tier 1 and carried over into Tier 2 supplemental instruction. Table 5.1, developed from information found in Graves (2008) and Mercer et al. (2011), provides an overview of each of the steps.

The writing process is dynamic in that the student author may return to a previous step if necessary (e.g., after the student begins the writing step he or she may need to return to the prewriting step in order to revise the writing plan

TABLE 5.1   Essential Components of the Writing Process

Component	Description	Key Tasks
Prewrite	Develop/explore initial ideas	Clarify purpose of writing task Brainstorm potential topics Identify intended audience Select writing topic List initial ideas for topic
Write Initial Draft	Begin composing	Generate rough draft Make certain initial ideas are included
Share	Share draft with peers or teacher	Read draft to others in small group Listen to feedback and ideas from others Record others' ideas and suggestions
Rewrite	Adjust content of written piece using feedback and own thoughts to more clearly state ideas	Generate second draft of material Reread to ensure all desired changes are made Compare material with stated purpose of assignment and adjust content as needed
Edit	Attend to proper writing mechanics	Review material to ensure that proper grammar, sentence structure, spelling, punctuation, capitalization, and handwriting (if handwritten) exist throughout Correct mechanics as needed
Evaluate	Perform final review prior to publishing	Proofread material to check for sufficient content, accuracy of statements, proper word usage, and correct mechanics throughout the entire composition Make any final necessary changes
Publish	Formal sharing of material	Present written material to others in one of several ways: publication in a newspaper or magazine, printing as a newsletter item, reading aloud, display on a board, submission as a formal written paper, etc.

or topic) (Graves, 2008). The seven steps within the writing process are typically embedded within Tier 1 writing curricula or programs. Adherence to these steps with fidelity is essential to establish necessary writing adjustments and to select effective evidence-based writing interventions, should Tier 2 instruction be warranted.

Foundational Elements of Effective Writing

In addition to steps in the overall writing process discussed, several elements serve as a foundation for delivering written instruction to all learners. These foundational aspects are considered essential to the success of any writing program (Pritchard & Honeycutt, 2007), must initially exist with fidelity in Tier 1 instruction, and must be continued in Tier 2 should this support be necessary.

ADDRESS EMOTIONAL ISSUES ■ Writing involves both skill and emotion to be successful. To address emotional aspects of writing, programs should facilitate a "positive, nonthreatening social climate" (Pritchard & Honeycutt, 2007, p. 31), in which students engage in writing on a daily basis. Guided practice, peer support, and sufficient opportunities are provided to help learners be more comfortable with writing tasks.

► **Struggling Writers:** Students who struggle with writing require additional support, encouragement, and opportunities to use various writing interventions to increase their success at addressing emotional issues in their writing.

UNDERSTANDING THE WRITING PROCESS ■ An effective writing program is grounded in a structured and defined process such as the one discussed. However, once it has been initiated, it is essential that students understand each step in the process and eventually comprehend the fact that collectively the individual steps lead to a finished writing product.

► **Struggling Writers:** "Teachers must demystify the writing process" (Pritchard & Honeycutt, 2007, p. 33) by teaching students about the process of writing, emphasizing that all good writers follow a similar process.

SELF-REGULATION STRATEGIES/STRATEGY INSTRUCTION ■ Effective writing includes the use of **self-regulated learning** strategies through which students monitor their own writing. The students self-initiate thoughts and actions in order to successfully complete the writing task (Zimmerman & Risenberg, 1997). This practice includes strategies such as accessing prior knowledge, conducting evaluation, or engaging in self-reflection. In addition to identifying and understanding the need for self-regulation in writing, effective writing programs teach students how to develop and use various strategies that prepare them to more independently complete the various steps in the writing process. Specific writing intervention strategies are presented in a subsequent section of this chapter.

► **Struggling Writers:** Learners who struggle with writing often are in great need of new and different self-regulated strategies, along with direct instruction to acquire, maintain, and generalize use of these strategies. Often, struggling writers have attempted all or most of the writing strategies used in the classroom with all learners, and their lack of progress with writing indicates that they need to learn and apply other strategies in the writing process. For many struggling writers, the use of other strategies developed through direct strategy instruction may initiate greater writing success.

DEVELOP PEER-MEDIATED LEARNING ■ Writing is completed within a broader social context, and student writers require peer interaction and support on a regular basis in the classroom. More specifically, Gere and Abbott (1985) found that effective writing occurs through interactions and conferencing with other writers, educators, and peers. As a result, the development of peer groups, cooperative **learning strategies**, and other peer-mediated strategies is essential to successful writing programs. The underlying premise in peer-mediated writing, such as use of peer response groups or peer partners, is that writing is best improved when the writer is responding to feedback reflecting specific criteria (Graham et al., 2007).

▶ **Struggling Writers:**   Papers written by students with disabilities " are shorter, incomplete, poorly organized, and weaker in overall quality" (Troia, 2006, p. 325). Although not all struggling writers have a disability, many of these same attributes of written expression are found in many struggling writers' works. Incorporating support and input from peers, provided in structured ways, allows struggling writers to acquire necessary insights, skills, and knowledge relative to the actual context of their writing samples. In addition, learners who struggle with writing are empowered as they, in turn, are able to provide others with support and feedback in a reciprocal manner.

Two key aspects (i.e., process and foundational elements) are necessary for successful writing to occur. Each of these aspects requires confirmation of implementation with fidelity should screening or progress-monitoring scores indicate lack of progress.

The purpose of this chapter is to identify selected writing interventions that educators should use within the parameters of the effective implementation of the foundational elements and the writing process. That is, we will discuss interventions that educators can use to assist struggling writers after the foundational elements and the writing process have both been implemented with fidelity and the learner continues to make inadequate progress. Developing written expression skills is a complex process requiring an integrated set of skills that typically are found in established writing programs implemented in Tier 1 instruction. For example, one popular and effective program is the Writer's Workshop Program (Lucy Calkins and Colleagues, Teachers College Columbia University), which guides students through various stages of writing. The reader is referred to the preceding sources and to Graham and Harris (2005); Harris, Graham, Mason, and Friedlander (2008); MacArthur, Graham, and Fitzgerald (2006); and Tompkins (2008) for detailed discussions about different writing programs for use in Tier 1 instruction. Key writing interventions to meet the needs of struggling learners, as supplemental to Tier 1 instruction and through Tier 2 or 3 instruction, are provided in the following sections.

Writing Interventions

After the writing process and foundational elements are in place and implemented properly, struggling writers benefit from additional supports that are designed to enhance their writing opportunities and outcomes. Struggling writers are identified through screening and progress-monitoring results. Table 5.2 presents an overview of each writing intervention in this chapter and is followed by a more detailed discussion to provide educators with the knowledge they need to deliver each intervention. The first intervention presented is an overall model, the Self-Regulated Strategy Development (SRSD) model, for assisting writers to develop various writing strategies. The model is followed by several interventions that may be developed adhering to its steps and procedures. Each of the interventions presented were selected due to their significance in guiding learners to success with different aspects of the writing process, including two learning strategies that directly facilitate self-regulated learning. *Evaluation* is an effective strategy to help students monitor their own learning through self-questioning. It is particularly useful in the complex process of writing, as is *Active Processing,* which helps writers tap into prior background knowledge (Hoover, 2011b; KU Center for Research on Learning website, 2011; Pritchard & Honeycutt, 2006). Evaluation and Active Processing complement each other and may be used together or individually, along with some of the other interventions discussed. In addition, the selected writing interventions may be used in conjunction with Tier 1 core curricula; most of the interventions require little formal

TABLE 5.2   Evidence-Based Writing Interventions

Writing Intervention	Keys to Writing
Self-Regulated Strategy Development Model	Teaches students to develop and use various writing strategies
Focus Correction Areas	Provides structure for revising written material in manageable and systematic ways
Report Writing Strategy	Guides students in prewriting activities by activating prior knowledge
Compare-Diagnose-Operate Strategy	Provides structured, stepwise approach for revising written material
Peer Revising Strategy	Provides peer-mediated structure for revising written material
Evaluation Strategy: Writing	Helps students to evaluate their own progress and outcomes related to the writing task
Active Processing: Writing	Helps students to access prior knowledge and skills pertaining to the writing topic

technical training and no or few additional curriculum materials, so they easily fit into existing Tier 1 core writing curriculum and instruction and may be used to provide supplemental Tier 2 supports.

Intervention: *Self-Regulated Strategy Development Model*

Primary Instructional Type	Primary Target Population	Primary Target Content Area(s)
_X_ Direct ____ Cooperative ____ Independent	The primary target population is the upper elementary through high school grades.	The primary target content is writing strategies.

INTERVENTION OVERVIEW ■ SRSD is a model used by educators to teach students how to use various writing strategies, particularly those strategies related to planning for and revising written material (Harris & Graham, 1996). Students using the SRSD model are taught self-regulating strategies in a variety of interrelated areas, including goal setting, monitoring work, and evaluating progress and products. The SRSD model components are illustrated in Table 5.3, which was developed from discussions found in Graham et al. (2007) and Graham and Harris (2005).

INSTRUCTIONAL USAGE ■ The SRSD model is used to teach students how to develop and use various writing strategies and interventions to employ the

TABLE 5.3   Components in the Self-Regulated Strategy Development Model

Component	Key Elements
1. Acquire Background Knowledge	Knowledge and skills necessary to understand, acquire, and employ writing strategies
2. Discuss It	Student's writing performance is cooperatively examined by the teacher and student One strategy to improve writing is identified
3. Model It	Teacher models selected writing strategy
4. Memorize It	With teacher support, student develops process for memorizing the strategy
5. Support It	Student is guided by teacher to apply strategy within context to complete writing task Peer-mediated support may also occur
6. Demonstrate Independent Performance	Student employs writing strategy on an independent basis to generalize to other writing tasks

writing process that was previously described (see Figure 5.1). That is, the SRSD model emphasizes "learning how to learn" through learning strategy development, such as the work on learning strategies completed at the University of Kansas. Each time a new writing strategy is presented to students, the teacher should follow the six steps outlined in Table 5.3, substituting the new strategy specifics to complete the process. By adhering to the steps in the SRSD model, students have a consistent and structured way to acquire, maintain, apply, and generalize a variety of writing strategies, including the strategies presented in the remainder of this chapter.

RESEARCH-BASED EVIDENCE ■ Graham et al. (2007) indicated that the SRSD model has been used with many students in more than 25 research projects. Research has found that this model is more effective for teaching students about strategy use than other strategy-development models (Graham & Perin, 2006; Harris & Graham, 1996).

EXPECTED LEARNER OUTCOME(S) ■ Through use of the SRSD model, learners become proficient in the use of various writing strategies and are able to improve their written material by applying the newly acquired strategy in a systematic way.

STEPS TO IMPLEMENTATION ■ Table 5.3 illustrated the six-step process for teaching students to improve their writing as they learn and apply new writing strategies. These steps are expanded on here to illustrate use in the classroom:

Step 1: Acquire Background Knowledge—Teacher guides the student to acquire the skills needed to best learn writing strategies. To meet this goal, teachers should follow several principles that are effective for teaching any strategy. These principles should be applied in Step 1 and in the subsequent steps as needed to ensure that the student successfully learns the strategy (Graham et al., 2007):

Principle 1: Explicitly teach the strategy by modeling its use and scaffolding learning.

Principle 2: Engage the student in an interactive process between teacher and student.

Principle 3: Be certain that the student possesses prerequisite skills that help with the strategy.

Principle 4: Individualize and personalize the strategy instruction to meet learner needs.

Principle 5: Provide sufficient time and practice so learner successfully acquires strategy.

Principle 6: Develop and sustain student motivation for learning and using new strategy.

Principle 7: Teach students self-monitoring methods to remind themselves to use the new strategy.

Principle 8: Ensure that the student is able to generalize the strategy to various writing situations.

By adhering to these principles, teachers can make sure that the students can more easily acquire the skills they need to apply different steps within the SRSD model.

Step 2: Discuss It—During this step, the teacher and student examine the student's writing and identify areas for improvement. The teacher suggests and discusses with the student a writing strategy that may help the learner improve a desired and agreed-on aspect of his or her writing. This strategy includes teaching the student procedures to self-monitor his or her own writing and revisions.

Step 3: Model It—The teacher models aloud the selected strategy using self-talk describing how the strategy is used. (An example of a learning strategy that employs self-talk is presented later in this chapter.) The student reflects on the teacher's self-talk and self-instructions. Together they discuss the strategy and personalize it to best fit the learner's needs. The student makes statements to self-regulate his or her own use of the strategy, which are documented, along with other prompts that will facilitate successful use of the strategy. Also during this stage, the teacher may model other uses of the strategy to ensure generalization to various writing tasks.

Step 4: Memorize It—During this step, the student memorizes the process for the strategy along with its intended meaning. (Refer back to Table 5.2 for examples of writing strategies.) Use of personalized statements developed in the previous step also assists with completion of Step 4. (See the Active Processing and Evaluation strategies discussed in the section that follows for examples of personalized statements.)

Step 5: Support It—Using guidance and support from the teacher and/or peers, the student applies the strategy in a writing assignment. The student attempts to employ the strategy and then discusses its effects on the writing task. The student receives both teacher and peer-mediated feedback and uses it until he or she is capable of applying the strategy on an independent basis.

Step 6: Independent Performance—The student applies the writing strategy independently to complete writing assignments. Teacher guidance, including the need to have the student establish a specific goal to use the strategy, is gradually withdrawn as the learner demonstrates mastery and generalization of the writing strategy.

IMPLEMENTATION FIDELITY CHECK ■ Fidelity in the use of the SRSD Model is maintained when the teacher and student successfully complete all six steps. In addition, the teacher should self-evaluate to confirm that the eight principles for teaching a writing strategy are embedded within the strategy development process.

INTERVENTION EFFECTIVENESS CHECKS ■ The SRSD model is designed to improve the quality of written material.

▶ **Progress-Monitoring Data Collection Device(s):** Use a writing probe.

▶ **Frequency of Monitoring Data Collection:** Collect data every 5–10 school days.

▶ **Diagnostic Assessment:** Use individual writing tests (e.g., Test of Written Language, Writing Process Test).

▶ **Lack of Progress (Intervention Adjustments):** Provide additional support to struggling learner to increase mastery of each of the six writing components. Pair struggling student with peer who has mastered the steps and have them jointly develop a written passage. Debrief with struggling writer, providing opportunity for student to reflect on use of each strategy. Provide struggling student with a template guiding use of the six writing Steps to Implementation. Support the teaching of each new writing strategy with visuals and a scaffolding process demonstrating effective use in actual writing assignments.

Intervention: *Focus Correction Areas*

Primary Instructional Type	Primary Target Population	Primary Target Content Area(s)
_X_ Direct ____ Cooperative ____ Independent	The primary target population is elementary and middle school grades.	The primary target content areas are written material revisions of drafts and final versions.

INTERVENTION OVERVIEW ■ The Focus Correction Area (FCA) intervention is a strategy by which the student is guided by the teacher to "focus" on select areas of the written material rather than attempting to revise multiple aspects of content and mechanics simultaneously (Collins, 1997). The FCA intervention allows students to focus their revisions on the content of the material first; then they focus on mechanics such as proper punctuation, capitalization, or sentence structure. An underlying concept is that often the initial focus on correcting mechanics does not lead to a higher quality written assignment; rather, initially addressing the select aspects of content is the more effective choice (Graham et al., 2007).

INSTRUCTIONAL USAGE ■ The FCA intervention is used when the goal is to provide structure for struggling writers in the process of revising their written material. This intervention is appropriate for use with elementary and middle school students who achieve the best results by directing their efforts to one or two revising areas at one time. The FCA intervention may be used for both small and large groups depending on the writing task.

RESEARCH-BASED EVIDENCE ■ The FCA intervention has been shown to enable struggling writers to more successfully complete initial to final drafts of a writing assignment (Graham et al., 2007). It is an effective method for use with struggling writers because it emphasizes delivering a more structured and directive method for providing revision-writing supports (Collins, 1997; Graham et al., 2007).

EXPECTED LEARNER OUTCOME(S) ■ Through use of FCA, learners develop written material that contains appropriately revised content and mechanics completed in a structured way.

STEPS TO IMPLEMENTATION ■ The implementation of the FCA follows a few simple steps, directed by the teacher:

1. Identify one or two content aspects within the written material that require revisions.

2. Ensure that the student is familiar with examples of the content elements (e.g., "Are all main ideas included? Is each main idea supported with an additional idea?").

3. Provide the student(s) opportunity to make revisions in the targeted content areas.

4. Review the revisions either through peer work or individually.

5. After initial content revisions have been made, the teacher directs the student to make additional needed content revisions, adhering to the preceding steps until all main content areas are addressed.

6. The teacher directs the student to make one or two mechanics revisions as needed (e.g., punctuation, structure), adhering to the preceding steps.

7. Complete the process until all needed mechanical writing aspects are properly revised.

8. Debrief with the student, discussing the process for revising both content and mechanics and helping the learner to internalize the process for future revisions.

An emphasis on the six traits typically addressed in writing programs provides the teacher with a structure for selecting various FCAs and directing the

TABLE 5.4   Six Traits and Focus Correction Areas

Writing Trait	Focus Area for Corrections
Ideas and Content	Revise material to include all needed content and related ideas
Organization	Provide guidance on the proper organization of the written material, emphasizing the proper sequence of main and supporting ideas
Voice	Guide writers to be in touch with their unique voice so that the learners' individual writing style, tone, and expression are shared in the written material Ensure that a consistent voice occurs throughout the written material
Word Choice	Direct writers to choose words that fit the context and purpose for the written material Support vocabulary development and use across genres
Sentence Fluency	Focus on sentence structure and syntax, including use of proper grammar, to express ideas in a fluent and coherent manner
Conventions	Follow proper mechanics of writing after all main and supporting content ideas have been addressed Meet organization and word usage expectations

student to generate a polished and complete writing assignment. Table 5.4, developed from information found in Graham et al. (2007), provides an overview of these traits for use as a guide in selecting appropriate FCAs.

IMPLEMENTATION FIDELITY CHECK ■ Fidelity of the use of FCAs is seen in the proper use of the guided and targeted supports provided to struggling writers, who often are overwhelmed by the various revision needs of most written material prior to submission and publication. Teachers may follow a simple checklist or rubric to ensure that fidelity in the use of this intervention exists.

INTERVENTION EFFECTIVENESS CHECKS ■ FCA is designed to improve revisions of written material.

▶ **Progress-Monitoring Data Collection Device(s):**   Use a writing probe.

▶ **Frequency of Monitoring Data Collection:**   Collect data every 5–10 school days.

▶ **Diagnostic Assessment:**   Use individual writing tests (e.g., Writing Process Test, Test of Written Expression).

▶ **Lack of Progress (Intervention Adjustments):**   Provide additional support to struggling learner to increase mastery of each of the six FCA writing traits. Pair struggling student with peer who has mastered the traits and have them jointly develop a written passage. Debrief with struggling writer, providing opportunity for student to reflect on use of each writing trait. Provide struggling student with a template guiding use of the eight writing Steps to Implementation. Support the teaching of each new writing trait with visuals and a scaffolding process, demonstrating effective use in actual writing assignments. Provide extended time to allow struggling writers to master each of the six FCA writing traits, focusing on each one individually until it is mastered prior to moving on to the next trait.

Intervention: *Report-Writing Strategy*

Primary Instructional Type	Primary Target Population	Primary Target Content Area(s)
_X_ Direct ____ Cooperative ____ Independent	The primary target population is elementary and middle school grades; this intervention is also appropriate in high school for learners experiencing initial writing needs.	The primary target content area is the initial development of a report or other written material.

INTERVENTION OVERVIEW ■ The Report-Writing Strategy is an intervention that guides individuals or groups of students in prewriting activities to activate their prior knowledge and generate needed content to be included in the writing assignment.

INSTRUCTIONAL USAGE ■ This intervention is used with students who are "able to generate and organize information from multiple sources" (Graham et al., 2007, p. 133). Also, graphic organizing such as concept mapping (see Chapter 4) is used to record and organize brainstorming ideas to be used in the writing assignment. The Report-Writing Strategy contains several interrelated skills and may become rather complex for some students, especially struggling writers (Graham et al., 2007). Adhering to the steps previously presented in the SRSD method provides teachers a structure for teaching this intervention by tailoring it to those students who require specific instruction in each of the main components, as illustrated in the five steps to implementation.

RESEARCH-BASED EVIDENCE ■ MacArthur, Schwartz, Graham, Molloy, and Harris (1996) described the process for this intervention and suggested that it takes up to six weeks for students to fully grasp the strategy. However, after they have acquired it, it is a valuable writing tool for subsequent writing assignments. In addition, Graham et al. wrote that through use of this intervention "the overall quality of students' reports improved, even for the struggling writers" (2007, p. 136).

EXPECTED LEARNER OUTCOME(S) ■ After completing the use of the Report-Writing Strategy, learners' written material is expected to contain the main ideas presented in proper sequence and relying on lists or concept maps of the ideas generated through brainstorming activities.

STEPS TO IMPLEMENTATION ■ The implementation of the Report-Writing Strategy follows a few simple steps directed by the teacher within the structure of the SRSD model (MacArthur et al., 1996):

Step 1: Students activate their prior knowledge by initially brainstorming ideas related to the topic. Generate a list of these ideas and identify other related information that they need to acquire to fill in knowledge or concept gaps about the topic.

Step 2: Using the list created in Step 1, students generate a concept map, ensuring that all ideas are included as either main or supporting content, including specific details.

Step 3: Using key sources such as the Internet, encyclopedias, interviews, or books, the students locate the material for the items requiring additional information. As students gather information from these sources, they record three types of items:

■ Specific information to be gathered by consulting the source

■ Main idea(s) about the topic gathered from the resource material, interview, etc.

■ Information that adds to or expands on the previously developed concept map, which they then revise

Step 4: After gathering and expanding on the necessary information to write the report, the students organize the ideas they have documented on their concept maps by listing in order the sequence in which each idea is to be included in the written material.

Step 5: Students generate their initial drafts, periodically stopping to ensure that the sequence is being implemented as designed and/or going back to gather additional information as necessary. They continue this process until they have completed the report.

As suggested, the Report-Writing Strategy contains several interrelated tasks (i.e., brainstorming, mapping, gathering additional information, organizing proper sequence). As a result, this intervention may take some learners, especially struggling writers, an extended period of time to master (e.g., 4–6 weeks) and they may need multiple opportunities to apply the strategy in writing assignments. However, after they have mastered it, the Report-Writing Strategy will be a valuable writing tool for all learners as they progress through school.

IMPLEMENTATION FIDELITY CHECK ■ Fidelity in the use of this intervention is determined by ensuring that the students: (a) have sufficient opportunities to practice it, (b) complete each of the five steps as designed, spending sufficient time to ensure a complete outcome, and (c) are given direct instruction in the use and application of each of the five steps, especially if they are struggling writers.

INTERVENTION EFFECTIVENESS CHECKS ■ The Report Writing Strategy is designed to improve initial development of written material.

► **Progress-Monitoring Data Collection Device(s):** Use a writing probe or Written Language Observation Scale.

► **Frequency of Monitoring Data Collection:** Collect data every five school days.

► **Diagnostic Assessment:** Use individual writing tests (e.g., Test of Written Language, Test of Early Written Language).

► **Lack of Progress (Intervention Adjustments):** Provide additional support to struggling learners to increase their mastery of each of the five Steps to Implementation. Pair a struggling student with a peer who has mastered the five steps and have them jointly develop a written passage. Debrief with struggling writer, providing opportunity for student to reflect on use of each writing step. Provide struggling student with a template guiding his or her use of the five writing Steps to Implementation. Support the teaching of each new writing step with visuals and a scaffolding process to break down various tasks that may be included in the use of the intervention (e.g., brainstorming; mapping).

Intervention: *Compare-Diagnose-Operate Revising Strategy*

Primary Instructional Type	Primary Target Population	Primary Target Content Area(s)
____ Direct ____ Cooperative _X_ Independent	The primary target population is upper elementary and middle school grades; this intervention is also appropriate for high school learners requiring additional support with revising written material.	The primary target content areas are revisions to initially developed written material.

INTERVENTION OVERVIEW ■ The Compare-Diagnose-Operate (CDO) Revising Strategy directs individual students to revise their written material sentence by sentence. Students identify where a revision may be required by

(a) comparing what is written with what they intended to convey (Compare),

(b) determining the problem with the sentence requiring revision (Diagnose), and

(c) selecting and implementing the revision (Operate). Students use a series of prescribed statements to assist them with clarifying why a particular sentence may require revision (see the section that follows).

INSTRUCTIONAL USAGE ■ The CDO Revising Strategy is used to focus the writer's attention on each individual sentence, thereby facilitating a structured and systemic approach for revising material. Supporting materials for this intervention require teachers to make several cards for use in the Diagnose and Operate steps (Graham, 1997):

Diagnose Cards (seven different cards):

> Doesn't sound right
>
> Not what I meant to say
>
> Not useful in my paper
>
> Good sentence
>
> Others may not understand what I am saying
>
> Others may not be interested in what I am saying
>
> Others may not believe what I am saying in this part

Operate Cards (four different cards):

> Rewrite
>
> Add more
>
> Delete this part
>
> Change the wording

Using these prompts, the writer revises the material one sentence at a time. The prompt cards allow the writer to see the sequence of ideas and ensure that they fit together as the revisions progress.

RESEARCH-BASED EVIDENCE ■ Graham (1997) validated the use and effectiveness of the CDO strategy with fifth and sixth graders who had learning disabilities. Results indicated that users of CDO revised more frequently and made more substantive revisions. Graham and Harris (2002) suggest that CDO is not appropriate for younger elementary students in the general classroom due to the complexities involved in use of the strategy. However, the "CDO procedure appears to be a useful tool for fourth through sixth grade children in general classrooms" (Graham & Harris, 2002, p. 73).

EXPECTED LEARNER OUTCOME(S) ■ After completing the use of the CDO Revising Strategy, learners in the upper elementary grades are expected to make more revisions than typically seen in these grades. Revisions are expected to be more accurate, thereby improving the written material.

STEPS TO IMPLEMENTATION ■ The implementation of the CDO Revising Strategy is completed by adhering to the following steps for each sentence (Graham, 1997):

Step 1: Compare—Student reads the sentence and determines whether it requires revising because it is unclear, needs expansion, and/or doesn't seem to fit the paper. (Note: If the sentence does not require revision, the student proceeds to the next sentence in the passage);

Step 2: Diagnose—If a revision is necessary, the student clarifies why the sentence needs revising by selecting the *Diagnose Card* that best reflects the reason.

Step 3: Operate—The student selects the one *Operate Card* that best defines how the sentence should be revised. The student makes the revision and puts the Diagnose and Operate cards back in their respective groups.

The process is completed for each sentence in the passage until all sentences have been addressed. Then the student rereads the entire piece to ensure that all revisions were made properly.

IMPLEMENTATION FIDELITY CHECK ■ Fidelity in the use of this intervention is determined by observing the student revise the written material sentence by sentence, adhering to the preceding three steps, including use of the Diagnose and Operate cards. The teacher may also check fidelity by discussing the process with the student to gather feedback about the use of the intervention and its components in revising written material.

INTERVENTION EFFECTIVENESS CHECKS ■ CDO is designed to improve revisions of written material.

▶ **Progress-Monitoring Data Collection Device(s):** Use a writing probe or Written Language Observation Scale.

▶ **Frequency of Monitoring Data Collection:** Collect data after completion of each writing assignment.

▶ **Diagnostic Assessment:** Use individual writing tests (e.g., Test of Written Expression, Test of Written Language).

▶ **Lack of Progress (Intervention Adjustments):** Provide additional support to struggling learner to increase mastery of each of the three Steps to Implementation. Pair struggling student with a peer who has mastered the three revision steps and have them jointly revise a written passage sentence by sentence. Debrief with struggling writer, providing opportunity for student to reflect on use of each of the three items (Compare, Diagnose, Operate). Provide struggling student with a template guiding use of the three items. Support the teaching of each new writing item with visuals and a scaffolding process demonstrating effective use in actual writing assignments. Provide extended time to allow struggling writer to focus on each of the three CDO writing strategies and master it before going on to the next.

Intervention: *Peer Revising Strategy*

Primary Instructional Type	Primary Target Population	Primary Target Content Area(s)
____ Direct _X_ Cooperative ____ Independent	The primary target population is the upper elementary and middle school grades; this intervention is also appropriate in high school for learners requiring revision peer supports.	The primary target content areas are revisions to initially developed written material.

INTERVENTION OVERVIEW ■ The Peer Revising Strategy provides students the opportunity to work with a peer to obtain feedback and ideas that are designed to support the revision of written material. This intervention includes two parts in which the student first focuses on revising the substance of the material, then gives attention to mechanics issues and needs (MacArthur, Schwartz, & Graham, 1991). The students work in pairs, assuming one of two roles: (a) writer, the author of the material, and (b) listener, who reads the material and provides feedback.

INSTRUCTIONAL USAGE ■ The Peer Revising Strategy is used to allow peers to "provide suggestions to each other on how to improve first drafts" (Graham & Harris, 2005, p. 63). This intervention is especially useful to struggling writers, including those with learning disabilities, who require more frequent revisions of written material. In addition, this intervention provides motivation for students to improve their written material within a positive social context.

RESEARCH-BASED EVIDENCE ■ This strategy has been directly validated for use with elementary students with learning disabilities in grades 4–6 in their work to generate and revise narrative text (MacArthur et al., 1991). Specifically,

Graham and Harris (2005) wrote that when it is used with students who have learning disabilities, the peer revising strategy positively affected revising behaviors and the quality of the written material. These authors also emphasized that these students made nearly three times as many revisions as did students who used more traditional revising methods. In addition, other researchers suggest that this intervention is appropriate and a valuable tool for use with elementary students ages 6–11 years (Nixon & Topping, 2001).

EXPECTED LEARNER OUTCOME(S) ■ After completing the use of the Peer Revising Strategy, learners are expected to make an increased number of meaningful revisions in both content and mechanics to their writing drafts, using feedback provided by peers.

STEPS TO IMPLEMENTATION ■ The implementation of the Peer Revising Strategy follows a few simple steps directed by the teacher (MacArthur et al., 1991):

1. Using the read-along method, the writer shares the draft of the written material with the listener by reading the paper aloud while the listener reads along silently.

2. During this initial reading, the listener is encouraged to ask questions to clarify ideas or sentences.

3. After completion of the read-along, the listener tells the writer what the main idea of the material is, what important ideas in the piece are, and which topics he or she most liked. This process ensures that the listener is attending to the task and provides the writer insight into how others perceive the content.

4. The listener then reads the paper, focusing on two tasks: clarity of the paper and identification of details that could be added. The listener records edits to address mechanics and word usage issues.

5. The listener offers three suggestions for adding details or clarifying the material, writing directly on the writer's paper.

6. The listener and writer discuss the suggestions and the writer includes the suggestions that he or she wishes to address in the next revision.

7. The listener shares edits to address mechanics and word usage issues after the content aspects have been discussed. (As with the FCA intervention, initial efforts are placed on the content aspects of the material, followed by consideration of mechanics revisions.)

8. The writer revises the material, addressing both content and mechanics discussed with the listener. After the piece is completed, the two get back together to consider the revisions and determine whether additional adjustments need to be made.

IMPLEMENTATION FIDELITY CHECK ▪ Fidelity in the use of this intervention is determined by observing that the pair of students adheres to the preceding steps in their discussions and that the writer incorporates the listener's content and mechanics suggestions into revised drafts. The teacher may also check fidelity by discussing the process with each pair to gather feedback about the use of the intervention.

INTERVENTION EFFECTIVENESS CHECKS ▪ The Peer Revising Strategy is designed to improve revisions of initial drafts of written material completed by peers.

▶ **Progress-Monitoring Data Collection Device(s):** Use a writing probe or Written Language Observation Scale.

▶ **Frequency of Monitoring Data Collection:** Collect data after completion of each writing assignment.

▶ **Diagnostic Assessment:** Use individual writing tests (e.g., Test of Written Expression, Test of Early Written Language).

▶ **Lack of Progress (Intervention Adjustments):** Provide additional support to struggling learner to increase mastery of each of the eight Steps to Implementation. Pair struggling student with a peer who has mastered the eight revision steps and have them jointly revise a written passage. Pair struggling student with peer who has mastered both roles of writer and listener. Pair struggling student with peer who jointly assumes the roles of writer and listener until the learner is able to implement them individually. Debrief with struggling writer, providing opportunity for student to reflect on each role and identify needed supports for improvement. Provide struggling student with a template guiding use of the two roles. Support the teaching of each new role with visuals and a scaffolding process, demonstrating effective use in actual writing assignments. Provide extended time to allow struggling writer to focus on each role individually until it is mastered prior to emphasizing the other role.

Intervention: *Evaluation Strategy: Writing*

Primary Instructional Type	Primary Target Population	Primary Target Content Area(s)
____ Direct	The primary target population is upper elementary and middle school grades; this intervention is also appropriate for high school learners who require additional supports in evaluating written work.	The primary target content area is the overall writing process.
____ Cooperative		
_X_ Independent		

INTERVENTION OVERVIEW ◼ The Evaluation Strategy: Writing intervention is the specific application of the broader self-monitoring and evaluation learning strategy applied to the complex task of written expression. This strategy assists writers to assume responsibility for their own learning through self-regulation. When evaluation is applied to the content area of written expression, it assists writers to become more aware of what needs to occur for them to successfully complete writing tasks. The strategy includes reflecting on the process and outcome of written assignments to ensure that they are completed properly, either individually and/or with the teacher. Evaluation reflects monitoring, which emphasizes use of self-questioning and is effective in helping students complete tasks (Deshler, Ellis, & Lenz, 1996).

INSTRUCTIONAL USAGE ◼ Evaluation Strategy: Writing is used to assist writers to self-monitor, reflect, predict, generalize, and accept feedback on aspects of writing tasks. This strategy is used to help writers gain greater control over learning by increasing their abilities to evaluate their own writing and to follow a specific process to complete writing tasks, thereby keeping them focused on the most essential aspects of the writing task.

RESEARCH-BASED EVIDENCE ◼ Evaluation is associated with self-monitoring and is found to be effective in helping students acquire greater control over their own learning (Deshler et al., 1996). Supporting research is summarized by Bender, who wrote that "a learning strategy may be thought of as a method of cognitively planning the performance of a learning task" (2009, p. 92). When it is applied within a written expression program, evaluation supports self-regulated learning, promotes independence, and provides a necessary structure to a complex process.

EXPECTED LEARNER OUTCOME(S) ◼ After completing the use of the Evaluation Strategy: Writing, learners in the upper elementary and middle school grades will achieve greater awareness of (a) their own writing skills and abilities, (b) the process they need to follow to successfully complete writing tasks, and (c) how to be successful with written expression through self-monitoring and reflection.

STEPS TO IMPLEMENTATION ◼ The implementation of the Evaluation Strategy: Writing follows a few simple steps to guide students' self-regulated writing, as described by Hoover (2011b):

> *Analysis:* "First, I will identify the process I will follow to complete my writing task. I will make certain that I have all necessary materials and I will estimate the amount of time needed to complete the task. What have I done recently that is similar to this assignment that will help me be suc-

cessful with this writing assignment? What does my completed writing task include? How will I know that I have completed my task?"

Strategy Identification: "What strategy (e.g., Report-Writing Strategy, CDO) will I use to complete my writing task? Why do I think this strategy will work? Do I understand the strategy well enough to use it to complete the task? Have I prioritized the ideas in the order that I need to include them in my writing? Have I selected my strategy?"

Implementation: "Before I begin I will review the process and strategy I will use to complete the writing task. Do I remember each of the steps to follow? I will follow the seven-step writing process and complete each selected strategy in the way that it was designed. If questions or issues arise as I am completing my task, I will ask for peer or teacher assistance."

Reflection: "As I am completing my writing task, I will periodically check to make certain that I am following the correct procedures and including the topic ideas in the proper order. If I find that the selected strategy is not working, I will try a different one. Is my process and selected strategy working to help me successfully complete my writing task? Am I confused about any aspect of the process or strategy?"

Generalization: "Did I complete my task? Does my final writing product contain all the key ideas I wanted to include? Have I revised my material using peer or teacher feedback? Am I pleased with my completed task? What did I learn about the process of writing and how can I use what I learned in future writing tasks?"

The writer considers each step in the course of developing and implementing the writing task, culminating in self-evaluation through reflection on and generalization of the process and written product. *Note*: The ideas presented in each step are types of examples and questions that students may use to guide their writing. Other statements or questions may be substituted to meet specific student evaluation needs.

IMPLEMENTATION FIDELITY CHECK ■ Fidelity in the use of this intervention is determined by observing the student address each step to develop and implement the writing task. The teacher may also devise a simple guide describing each step, which the teacher and student may complete either during or after completion of the writing task as another fidelity check, such as the one illustrated in Form 5.1 at the end of this text.

INTERVENTION EFFECTIVENESS CHECKS ■ Evaluation Strategy: Writing is designed to improve the quality of written material.

▶ **Progress-Monitoring Data Collection Device(s):** Use a writing probe or Written Language Observation Scale.

- ▶ **Frequency of Monitoring Data Collection:** Collect data after completion of each writing assignment.

- ▶ **Diagnostic Assessment:** Use individual writing tests (e.g., Test of Written Language, Test of Written Expression).

- ▶ **Lack of Progress (Intervention Adjustments):** Provide additional support to struggling learner to increase mastery of each of the five Evaluation items in the Steps to Implementation. Pair struggling student with a peer who has mastered the five Evaluation Steps and have them jointly apply each step to a written assignment. Debrief with struggling writer, providing opportunity for student to reflect on use of each of the Evaluation Strategy steps. Provide struggling student with a template guiding implementation of the Evaluation Strategy: Writing process. Support the teaching of each of the five Evaluation Strategy: Writing steps with visuals and a scaffolding process, demonstrating effective use in actual writing assignments (e.g., document steps on flash cards for future reference).

Intervention: *Active Processing: Writing*

Primary Instructional Type	Primary Target Population	Primary Target Content Area(s)
____ Direct ____ Cooperative _X_ Independent	The primary target population is the upper elementary through high school grades.	The primary target content areas are prewriting and initial writing tasks.

INTERVENTION OVERVIEW ■ Active Processing: Writing is a strategy that contains a set of procedures for assisting writers to access their prior knowledge and elaborate on that knowledge to frame the new writing task, particularly during its development. Like the previous strategy, evaluation, active processing employs self-talk and questioning that is completed individually or with teacher guidance to identify what the students currently know about the writing topic, simultaneously confirming that they understand the requirements of the task at hand.

INSTRUCTIONAL USAGE ■ The Active Processing: Writing strategy is used during the prewriting and initial writing steps of the writing process. (See Figure 5.1.) Clarifying existing knowledge about an upcoming task or topic increases the writer's ownership, motivation, and ability to complete the task.

RESEARCH-BASED EVIDENCE ■ The Active Processing: Writing strategy reflects research results that emphasize the significance of drawing on background or prior knowledge (i.e., KWL: What I KNOW; What I WANT to know; What I LEARNED) as learners engage in new writing tasks (Chapman & King, 2003; Pritchard & Honeycutt, 2006).

EXPECTED LEARNER OUTCOME(S) ■ After completing the use of Active Processing: Writing, learners will have drawn on their prior knowledge in the development and completion of the writing task and will appreciate the importance of building on existing knowledge to acquire new learning.

STEPS TO IMPLEMENTATION ■ The implementation of Active Processing: Writing follows a few simple steps, as described by Hoover (2011b):

> *Define:* "To begin I need to clarify what I am expected to do to complete the task. What ideas or items need to be included in the writing material? What do I already know about this topic?"
>
> *Activate:* "Determine what I have used in previous similar writing assignments. How might what I already know about this task or topic help me complete the writing assignment?"
>
> *Specify and Plan:* "How should I structure the task to be sure all ideas or items are included? What aspects of this task will be easier for me to complete using my background knowledge of the topic? I will list the steps I need to follow to complete the task."
>
> *Check:* "Am I following the steps I established to implement the task? Am I using what I already know about the topic to help me complete the task? How am I incorporating what I already know into the new task?"
>
> *Monitor:* "Is my plan working? If not I will adjust it to better complete the assignment. How could an alternate plan address the issues that have arisen?"
>
> *Complete:* "Have I completed my task? What parts of my original plan worked? What parts did not work? How did my prior knowledge about the writing process or topic help me complete the task?"
>
> *Note*: The ideas presented in each step are types of examples and questions students may use to active their prior knowledge. Other statements or questions may be substituted to meet specific student active processing needs.

IMPLEMENTATION FIDELITY CHECK ■ Fidelity in the use of this intervention is determined by observing the student address each step as the writing task is developed and implemented. The teacher may also devise a simple guide describing each step, to be completed by the teacher and student either during or after completion of the writing task as another fidelity check, such as the one illustrated in Form 5.2 at the end of this text.

INTERVENTION EFFECTIVENESS CHECKS ■ Active Processing: Writing is designed to improve quality of written material, particularly during the pre-writing stage.

▶ **Progress-Monitoring Data Collection Device(s):** Use a writing probe or Written Language Observation Scale.

▶ **Frequency of Monitoring Data Collection:** Collect data on completion of each writing assignment.

▶ **Diagnostic Assessment:** Use individual writing tests (e.g., Test of Written Expression, Test of Language Development).

▶ **Lack of Progress (Intervention Adjustments):** Provide additional support to a struggling learner to increase mastery of each of the six Active Processing items in the Steps to Implementation. Pair a struggling student with a peer who has mastered the six Active Processing Steps and have them jointly apply each step to a written assignment. Debrief with struggling writer, providing opportunity for student to reflect on use of each of the Active Processing Steps to Implementation in the writing task. Provide struggling student with a template guiding implementation of the Active Processing: Writing procedures. Support the teaching of each of the six Active Processing: Writing steps with visuals and a scaffolding process, demonstrating effective use in actual writing assignments.

Comprehensive Writing Programs

A key strength in using the preceding EBIs is that they may be used along with or supplemental to a variety of comprehensive Tier 1 core writing curricula that already are in use in the classroom. The writing interventions described in this chapter require little or no purchasing of separate materials, which makes them highly usable and functional for most classrooms where writing needs require additional supports. Although many comprehensive reading programs also include writing program components, there are several writing programs that may be used to implement multi-tiered instruction. Several of these writing programs are summarized in Table 5.5. These programs are comprehensive and include necessary materials, activities, supports, enrichment, and core instruction in the key writing instructional areas of content and mechanics (e.g., conventions, process, fluency, vocabulary usage). These programs may be expensive and may not be available in different schools; they are listed in order to share the key aspects of the programs, and the reader is referred to each program's citation for additional information.

TABLE 5.5 Comprehensive Writing Programs for Elementary and Middle School

Program	Brief Description
Success for All (Writing Wings) (Success for All Foundation, 2010)	Teaches students in grades 3–5 the writing process, focusing on writing ideas, organization, style, and mechanics
The Units of Study for Primary Writing: A Yearlong Curriculum Series (K–2) (Lucy Calkins and Colleagues, Heinemann, 2010)	Primary writer's workshop program for elementary students in grades K–2, teaching the developmental stages of writing. Contains seven units of study
Units of Study for Teaching Writing, Grades 3–5 (Lucy Calkins and Colleagues, Heinemann, 2010)	Upper elementary writer's workshop program for students in grades 3–5, teaching narrative and expository writing. Contains six units of study
Language for Writing (Engelmann & Osborn, 2003)	Direct instruction program for teaching students in grades 2–5 to communicate effectively through written language. Program is a revised version of the Distar Language III program
Apple Tree Curriculum for Developing Written Language (2nd ed.) (Pro-Ed, 1999)	Provides students in lower elementary grades who have a language impairment a structured sequence of procedures for the construction and development of basic English sentence structures
Teaching Competence in Written Language: A Systematic Program for Developing Writing Skills (2nd ed.) (Pro-Ed, 2000)	Program for learners in grades 3–12 that provides a step-by-step, structured hierarchy of writing skills, from the most basic to advanced
Write Connection (write-connection.com)	Comprehensive program that teaches essential components that students need in order to become effective writers

Strategies for Differentiated Writing Instruction

In addition to comprehensive RBCs and the structured evidence-based writing interventions, there exist numerous teaching and student strategies to ensure implementation of a differentiated classroom. A variety of techniques that are student-directed were presented in Table 2.2, including several techniques that are specific to differentiating writing instruction to prevent learner needs from becoming more significant. Unlike the more highly structured EBIs that were previously presented, these student strategies are simple techniques that typically require little prior training and that are easily incorporated into any classroom structure, Tier 1 core curriculum, or Tier 2 supplemental supports. Table 5.6 provides a list of writing strategies previously presented in Chapter 2 to remind the reader of appropriate writing-based differentiations. The reader is referred to Table 2.2 for a review of each writing strategy.

As shown, several easy-to-use writing strategies exist to improve various aspects of written expression. Although the strategies are not all-inclusive, their

TABLE 5.6 Strategies for Differentiating Writing Instruction

Writing Strategy	Focus Area
COPS	Proofreading
DEFENDS	Written expression
NEAT	Overall appearance
PENS	Sentence writing
REAP	Integrates reading and writing
STOP	Brainstorming/Prewriting planning

use in a differentiated writing instruction environment may prevent writing needs from becoming more significant, reducing the need for more resource-intensive Tier 2 instruction. In addition, should Tier 2 instruction in writing be warranted, these strategies may be continued to further differentiate instruction for struggling writers.

CONCLUSION

Written expression is a highly complex skill requiring ongoing practice, instruction, and feedback. The need to adjust instruction to accommodate diverse writing abilities in today's classrooms challenges most teachers. The effects of increased uses of technology, varied experiential backgrounds, and ranges of reading abilities within the same classroom necessitates a creative and differentiated writing program to meet all needs. Any effective writing program must be (a) grounded in the teaching and learning of the writing process, (b) implemented daily, and (c) structured to facilitate active engagement among peers and teachers. Struggling writers are identified early through screening and progress monitoring, and EBIs are implemented to support their writing needs. This text presented several interventions, along with existing differentiated strategies and comprehensive writing programs. Educators who establish and maintain a structured and well-guided writing program (e.g., writer's workshop) will find the models and practices presented in this chapter to be highly useful tools to support their written expression programs in any tier of instruction.

Instructions: Complete each item prior to or during completion of the writing task.

1. *Analysis:* State the materials and other information needed to complete the writing task.

2. *Strategy Identification:* Identify the strategy to be used to successfully complete the writing task, listing the steps that you will follow and stating why the strategy will help with task completion.

3. *Implementation:* Either with another peer or with a teacher, verbally review the strategy to make certain you understand the process as you begin to implement it, following the proper steps.

4. *Reflection:* State how you will periodically check to make sure the selected strategy is working and to make any adjustments you need to keep progressing toward completing the writing task.

5. *Complete:* State how you will know that the task is complete and that all important ideas are included in the final product.

Summary: Summarize how the selected strategy worked and how it may be used again in future writing assignments.

Instructions: Complete each item prior to or during completion of the writing task.

1. *Define:* State the writing task and what you intend to accomplish.

2. *Activate:* Develop a list of ideas that you have used in the past to complete a similar writing task.

3. *Specify/Plan:* List the steps that you will follow to complete the writing task.

4. *Check:* State how you will check to make sure steps are implemented properly to complete writing task.

5. *Monitor:* State what you will look for to be sure the plan and steps being implemented are working and help-ing to complete the writing task.

6. *Complete:* State how you will know that the task is complete.

Summary: Summarize what worked and did not work in the plan and describe the adjustments you made.

CHAPTER 6

Evidence-Based Mathematics Practices

▶ **Chapter Overview**

TEACHING MATHEMATICS IS AS complex as teaching reading or writing. Mathematics instruction requires educators to implement a structured program to develop students' mastery of both content and process standards. Effective mathematics instruction emphasizes an integrated set of skills, such as fluency, problems solving, communication, and reasoning, grounded in the National Council of Teachers of Mathematics (NCTM) standards. This chapter provides an overview of mathematics education elements that must be present in effective multi-tiered instruction, strategies for differentiating mathematics instruction, and selected mathematics interventions and programs to meet Tier 1, 2, and 3 instructional needs of struggling learners.

Key Terms

- Abstract
- Computation
- Concrete
- Differentiated mathematics instruction
- NCTM Standards
- Reasoning
- Semiconcrete

Mathematics Content Areas and Multi-Tiered Instructional Interventions

Mathematics Content Skill Areas

Select a mathematics intervention that targets the assessed content area in which the learner demonstrates inadequate mathematics progress.

Mathematics Interventions	Operations/Facts	Word Problems	Structured Math Process
Schema-Based Instruction (SBI)		X	
Concrete-Semiconcrete-Abstract (CSA)			X
Unitary, Decade, Sequence, Separate, Integrated Model (UDSSI)	X		
Cognitive Guided Instruction (CGI)		X	
Classwide Peer Tutoring–Mathematics (CWPT)			X
Peer-Assisted Learning Strategies-Mathematics (PALS)			X
MATHFACT	X		

Foundation of Mathematics Instruction

Initially, mathematics instruction drew clear lines of distinction between the elementary and secondary grades. **Computation** and word problems were taught in elementary school, and algebra and geometry were taught in secondary school. Although these areas of emphasis still exist, today's K–12 mathematics instruction uses a more integrated approach, blending both content and process skills and using the **National Council of Teachers of Mathematics (NCTM) Principles and Standards for School Mathematics** (NCTM, 2000). Over the past several decades, the field of mathematics has adopted programs

Standards	Key Components
Content	Mathematics topical areas that shape operations and elements taught in elementary and secondary school
Number and Operations	Basic mathematical operations and number correspondence (e.g., addition, subtraction, one-to-one correspondence)
Algebra	Symbolic reasoning, calculations with symbols
Geometry	Measurement/relationships (e.g., shapes, lines, points)
Measurement	Connected to geometry; includes study of various concepts (e.g., length, depth, time, money, volume)
Data Analysis/Probability	Study and interpretation of visuals such as charts and graphs; understanding of data analysis and probability
Process	Mathematical processes necessary to apply content knowledge taught in elementary and secondary school
Problem-Solving	Abilities to solve mathematics word problems
Reasoning and Proof	Skills necessary to solve problems, evaluate solutions, and acquire new skills, requiring careful and systematic reasoning, proofing, and justification abilities
Communication	Use of mathematical language to communicate process and results to demonstrate logical thinking, analysis, and organization
Connections	Abilities to connect mathematical ideas and concepts across domains, such as use of algebra, geometry, or measurement knowledge to build new skills or clarify patterns (e.g., temperature patterns in a dry region)
Representation	Use of various forms of expression to communicate mathematics (e.g., numbers, equations, graphs, algebraic symbols)

that reflect the new math movement, the back-to-basics movement, and the contemporary integrated movement, in which both content and process standards are addressed to some degree in each grade level (Haager & Klingner, 2005). Table 6.1, developed from information found in Cohen and Spenciner (2009) and NCTM (2000), illustrates the 10 NCTM mathematics standards that are emphasized in today's Tier 1 mathematics curricula and associated EBIs.

A high-quality research-based Tier 1 core mathematics curriculum includes a program that teaches toward mastery of these 10 standards in an organized and structured manner. Content and process skills related to each standard are taught in integrated ways throughout grades K–12.

Mathematics and Use of Mental Processes

According to Seethaler and Fuchs (2006), mathematics requires learners to use a variety of mental skills, including those reflecting mental **reasoning**, processing, concept formation, or memory. Bender wrote "math is a highly complex skill that rests on many other brain functions" (2009, p. 4). In addition, students who struggle with mathematics, including those with learning disabilities, often exhibit problems with using calculation strategies, lack mathematics fluency, and possess poor memory usage abilities (Bender, 2009; Woodward, 2006). As a result, the acquisition, maintenance, and generalization of mathematics requires the student to use various brain functions, which, in turn, require differentiated instruction to assist learners to access and apply needed mental processes.

Attention to various strategies becomes especially important for learners who struggle with mathematics, as these students may need interventions that require additional use of mental functions to accommodate possible disabilities or other mathematics learning problems. Researchers have identified several guidelines for teachers to ensure that their students are effectively using a variety of mental processes when they are learning mathematics. Several of these guidelines are presented in Table 6.2. The table was developed from information found in Bender (2009), reflecting several general suggestions for classroom consideration. These suggestions are referred to as brain-compatible guidelines and are not the only appropriate guidelines. Incorporation of these techniques when determining Tier 1 mathematics instructional fidelity or the selection of Tier 2 interventions facilitates the implementation of effective multi-tiered instruction for students who struggle with mathematics. For a more detailed discussion and additional guidelines, the reader is referred to Bender (2009).

TABLE 6.2 Guidelines for Facilitating Brain-Compatible Mathematics Instruction

Guideline	Description
Depth versus Breath	It may be preferable to help students with math problems acquire a more in-depth understanding of a topic by completing several problems that are similar, rather than requiring them to complete many math problems of varying types to learn the skill or concept.
Multi-level Presentation	New mathematical concepts or skills should be taught within three levels: (a) concrete, (b) representational or semiconcrete, and (c) abstract.
Big Ideas/Patterns	Effective mathematics instruction helps learners acquire big ideas and patterns that are found across different types of problems or skills that lead to effective ways to grasp math concepts.
Automaticity	Mathematics facts should be taught to a high level of fluency and automatic recall.
Novelty/Creativity	Mathematics instruction that includes new and creative ways to help students acquire new knowledge and skills provides for increased motivation and retention.
Scaffold Instruction	New mathematical concepts are best taught by emphasizing varying levels of difficulty structured through scaffolding of instruction by activating prior knowledge and tapping into learners' experiential backgrounds (i.e., begin with what the students currently know, build in supports to ease into new or complex concepts/skills, progress to more complex levels, and withdraw supports as independent learning evolves).

As shown, the guidelines facilitate a dynamic and creative structure for teaching mathematics to all students. Placing a specific emphasis on these and related teaching ideas with struggling learners can help them use various mental processes to increase their motivation, retention, and mastery of material. The next section provides discussion about several mathematics models and interventions that assist struggling learners to be more successful in acquiring, maintaining, and generalizing mathematics concepts and skills.

Evidence-Based Mathematics Instruction

A mathematics research-based comprehensive program is often found in classrooms (e.g., Saxon Math, Math Their Way, Investigations) and serves as the cornerstone of mathematics Tier 1 core instruction. Often, many of the instructional adjustments that are required to meet the needs of struggling learners are seen in the implementation of differentiated instruction (see Chapter 2), where existing math strategies are expanded on or new strategies are developed. However, some struggling students need to go beyond that which is provided in the core comprehensive curriculum and receive associated differentiations in the Tier 1 instruction. Several of the more frequently discussed interventions or models for teaching mathematics are briefly presented in Table 6.3 and discussed in detail in the sections that follow. Each of these models contain established steps or some defined process that enable educators to build on the existing curricula and differentiations by providing the necessary mathematical supports that typically are required in Tier 2 instruction.

TABLE 6.3 Evidence-Based Mathematics Interventions and Models

Mathematics Intervention	Description
Schema-Based Instruction	Use of schematic diagrams to teach complex math word problems
Concrete-Semiconcrete-Abstract	Teaching sequence designed to structure tasks that progress from the concrete to the abstract in a systematic manner
Unitary, Decade, Sequence, Separate, Integrated Model	Sequential process for learning early operations and higher level mathematics problems
Cognitive Guided Instruction	Use of teacher questioning to "guide" a learner through math problem-solving
Classwide Peer Tutoring-Mathematics	Application of CWPT in the guided and independent phases of mathematics instruction
Peer-Assisted Learning Strategies-Mathematics	Peer-mediated process to supplement core mathematics curricula for struggling learners
MATHFACT	Guidelines for helping students with learning problems acquire basic mathematics facts

The selected mathematics interventions may be used in conjunction with Tier 1 core curricula. Most require little formal technical training and no additional curriculum materials, so they easily fit into existing Tier 1 core mathematics curriculum and instruction.

Intervention: *Schema-Based Instruction*

Primary Instructional Type	Primary Target Population	Primary Target Content Area(s)
__X__ Direct ____ Cooperative ____ Independent	The primary target population is students struggling with word problems in grades 3–12.	The primary target content area is complex mathematics problems.

INTERVENTION OVERVIEW ■ Schema-based instruction (SBI) is based on the theory that students need to acquire a conceptual understanding of math problems rather than simply relying on procedures and rules (Maccini & Gagnon, 2002; Xin, Jitendra, & Deatline-Buchman, 2005). SBI emphasizes the use of a "conceptual teaching approach that integrates mathematical problem-solving and reading comprehension strategies" (Jitendra, 2008, p. 20). It employs teacher-mediated instruction that uses schematic diagrams to represent the important information in a math problem. The overall result is greater comprehension of the problem, leading to increased problem-solving performance.

INSTRUCTIONAL USAGE ■ SBI is used with learners who experience difficulty learning and solving complex mathematical word problems, including students with learning disabilities (Jitendra, 2008). SBI provides scaffolding of instruction for learners who require these types of supports through directed teaching using explicit instructions and self-regulated strategies. By going beyond simple procedures and rules to include visual design and semantic clues, SBI assists learners to experience greater success with word problems.

RESEARCH-BASED EVIDENCE ■ When it was compared with a more typical general method for teaching word problems, SBI was found to increase student performance. Xin et al. found that SBI was significantly more effective than general strategy instruction "on all measures of acquisition, maintenance and generalization" (2005, p. 189). Jitendra (2008) found that SBI is a promising mathematical intervention, and Bender (2009) wrote that SBI has been found to be effective with students in third grade and up.

EXPECTED LEARNER OUTCOME(S) ■ Through use of SBI, learners are expected to improve their abilities to solve more complex mathematics word problems, eventually becoming capable of independently completing complex word problems.

STEPS TO IMPLEMENTATION ■ Implementation of SBI requires initial teacher direction, followed by student application. The strategy must adhere to the following steps, as summarized from discussions found in Bender (2009), Jitendra (2008), and Xin et al. (2005):

1. Teach or review procedures for developing a schematic representation (i.e., diagram, map).

2. Assist learners to identify the requested outcome of the word problem. This will include one of three choices: (1) Change—problems that tell a story describing a situation requiring the learner to identify the change described; (2) Group—problems that result in distinct items or groups forming a new group or set; and (3) Compare—problems that require the learner to compare two numbers, such as figuring out how much older one person is than another. Here is an example derived from discussions in Bender (2009): "Is the problem asking you to *change, group,* or *compare* items?" The teacher illustrates each type of requested outcome as follows:

Change Outcome: Tom has several chairs for use in his home recital. Sue gave Tom 25 chairs, and now Tom has a total of 35 chairs. How many chairs did Tom have initially?

Unknown item (Tom's initial number of chairs ⟶ 25 chairs given to Tom by Sue ⟶ Tom now has 35 chairs

This visual diagram illustrates that the student should solve the problem for the beginning unknown item (i.e., Tom's initial chair count), by using subtraction (i.e., $35 - 25 = 10$).

Group Outcome: John has five different baseball caps and his friend Tom has seven different caps. When John and Tom combine their cap collections, from how many can they choose?

John–5 caps ⟶ Tom–7 caps ⟶ Unknown item (number of caps from which both may choose)

This visual diagram illustrates that the student should solve the problem for the unknown number of items by grouping them, by using addition (i.e., $5 + 7 = 12$).

Comparison Outcome: Sam has eight faves on his cell phone, four more than George. How many faves does George have?

Sam (8) ⟶ (4) More than George ⟶ Unknown (number of faves for George)

This visual diagram illustrates that the student should solve the problem for the unknown number of total faves for George, by using subtraction to compare values (i.e., $8 - 4 = 4$).

---

3. The student completes the unknown item in the visual schematic diagram by solving the problem.

4. The student repeats the process until he or she is able to successfully

    a. Identify the proper type of required schema found in simple word problems such as those illustrated (Change, Group, Comparison).

    b. Generate his or her own schematic visual of simple word problems.

    c. Solve a problem by completing or filling in the "unknown" variable.

5. After the student has learned how to use schematic diagrams to solve simple word problems, the teacher introduces more complex problems that require a two-step process to solve. The student uses Primary and Secondary Schema to solve the Problem Equation (Bender, 2009):

    Two-Step Problem: Sam has 8 chairs. Sid gives him 10 more chairs. Sam now has 5 more chairs than does Fred. How many chairs does Fred have?

Primary (Comparison Outcome)

Sam's chairs after Sid's contribution (A) ⟶ Difference in number of chairs between Sam and Fred (5 chairs) ⟶ Fred's chairs (unknown)

Problem Equation

A (Sam's chairs) − 5 (Difference: Sam/Fred) = Unknown (Fred's chairs)

Secondary (Change Outcome)

Chairs initially held by Sam − 8 ⟶ Number of chairs given to Sam − 10 ⟶ Sam's chairs − 18 (A)

After the student has developed the *Primary Schematic* visual, he or she generates the Problem Equation, which leads to the *Secondary Schematic* visual. Using the result from the *Secondary Schema* design (i.e., the solution for the A value), the student inserts the A value into the *Primary Schematic* design and uses subtraction to solve for the unknown in the Problem Equation (i.e., the number of chairs owned by Fred).

6. As in the case of the simple word problems, this process is directed by the teacher using scaffolding and explicit instruction until the student is able to successfully generate his or her own schemas to solve more complex mathematics word problems.

IMPLEMENTATION FIDELITY CHECK ■ Fidelity in the use of this intervention is determined by observing the student develop and use schematic diagrams to solve math problems. The teacher may also check fidelity by discussing the process with the student to gather feedback about the use of the intervention and its components in solving math problems.

INTERVENTION EFFECTIVENESS CHECKS ■ SBI is designed to improve students' abilities to solve mathematical word problems.

▶ **Progress-Monitoring Data Collection Device(s):** Use a mathematics probe.

▶ **Frequency of Monitoring Data Collection:** Collect data every five school days.

▶ **Diagnostic Assessment:** Use individual mathematics tests (e.g., Test of Mathematical Abilities, Comprehensive Mathematical Abilities Test).

▶ **Lack of Progress (Intervention Adjustments):** Provide additional support to struggling learners to increase mastery of the two schematics (primary and secondary) by ensuring that the learners have mastered each individually prior to combining the schematics. Pair a struggling student with a peer who has mastered the Steps to Implementation of SBI and have them jointly apply the Steps to several mathematics word problems. Debrief with struggling learner, providing opportunity for student to reflect on the problem tasks (i.e., Change, Group, or Comparison Outcome) requested in different mathematics problems. Provide struggling student with a template guiding determination of selection of appropriate outcome. Instruct struggling student to develop numerous simple examples of each type of requested outcome to develop mastery. Support the teaching of the two schematics with visuals and a scaffolding process, demonstrating effective use in mathematical word problems.

Intervention: *Concrete-Semiconcrete-Abstract Sequence*

Primary Instructional Type	Primary Target Population	Primary Target Content Area(s)
_X_ Direct ____ Cooperative ____ Independent	The primary target population is mathematics students, including struggling learners, in grades K–12.	The primary target content area is any mathematics content area.

INTERVENTION OVERVIEW ■ The Concrete-Semiconcrete-Abstract (CSA) intervention sequence is a process for teaching mathematical computational and problem-solving skills that guides the learner from the concrete to the abstract in a systematic manner (Mercer, Mercer, & Pullen, 2011). The CSA sequence (a) begins with a hands-on, tactile element (**concrete**), (b) proceeds to use illustrations or drawings moving off the tactile element only (**semiconcrete**), and (c) ends by completing the problem without the use of objects or illustrations (**abstract**). The systematic progression from the concrete to the abstract "enables students to understand the concepts of math prior to memorizing facts, algorithms and operations" (Mercer et al., 2011, p. 420).

INSTRUCTIONAL USAGE ■ The CSA model is appropriate for use with any learner and should serve as the foundation for teaching all computation and problem-solving skills in any grade. It can meet the learning needs of students who are struggling with various mathematics concepts, especially when they are making connections between equations and word problems, equations and objects, and illustrations and equations, as well as learning basic mathematics facts (Mercer et al., 2011).

RESEARCH-BASED EVIDENCE ■ Spangler (2010) wrote that some researchers (e.g., Bruner, 1996) suggest that students who use these three components are more successful with learning mathematics. In addition, "Miller and Hudson (2007) found that this type of three-stage model helps students with learning disabilities master concepts involving whole numbers, fractions and algebra" (Spangler, 2010, p. 6). In support, Mercer et al. (2011) wrote that use of the CSA model has been found to help students with learning problems acquire math facts.

EXPECTED LEARNER OUTCOME(S) ■ Learners taught through use of the CSA intervention sequence are expected to obtain a greater grasp of mathematical concepts that helps them complete computational and problem-solving tasks.

STEPS TO IMPLEMENTATION ■ The CSA intervention sequence follows the same easy-to-implement process for teaching any mathematics skill:

Step 1: Concrete—During this initial step, students use concrete aids by moving objects that accurately represent the math process being studied. The manipulative aids must reflect the same paper–pencil task process. The concrete learning experience occurs as the student manipulates or moves the objects to reflect the task, concept, or skill. During this step, the teacher asks the student questions about his or her actions and encourages the student to use self-talk or think aloud to verbalize what he or she is thinking as the objects are manipulated. This step should be repeated until the student demonstrates a grasp of the concrete aspects of the math task and is able to successfully solve the math problem using concrete manipulative materials.

Step 2: Semiconcrete—After the learner has demonstrated success at solving mathematics problems at the concrete level, he or she moves to the second stage, in which concrete objects are no longer used. In this stage, the student solves mathematics problems by using visual representations, such as diagrams, pictures, or lines. During this step, students use these visuals, rather than concrete manipulative materials, as supports to solve math problems. As in Step 1, the teacher should ask the student questions about what he or she is doing and thinking as the student uses the semiconcrete aspects to solve the mathematics problems.

Step 3: Abstract—After the student is able to solve problems using illustrations only (i.e., no concrete items), he or she is ready for the abstract aspect of this sequence. Students who are successful in this step are able to look at, read, and solve the problem without using concrete objects or visual illustrations. The ability to solve problems in the abstract is the ultimate goal. However, some students may need to return to the use of concrete and/or illustrations periodically when they encounter new mathematical problems, concepts, and skills. Teachers should allow them to do this.

IMPLEMENTATION FIDELITY CHECK ■ Fidelity in the implementation of CSA is determined by having the teacher observe student performance and ensure that learners have mastered each of the three elements in sequence. The teacher may develop and complete a simple checklist as the learner engages in the mathematics tasks that are associated with each of the three elements in the CSA intervention sequence.

INTERVENTION EFFECTIVENESS CHECKS ■ The CSA model is designed to improve overall achievement in mathematics.

▶ **Progress-Monitoring Data Collection Device(s):** Use a mathematics probe.

▶ **Frequency of Monitoring Data Collection:** Collect data every five school days.

▶ **Diagnostic Assessment:** Use individual mathematics tests (e.g., Test of Mathematical Abilities, Comprehensive Mathematical Abilities Test).

▶ **Lack of Progress (Intervention Adjustments):** Provide struggling learner numerous mathematics examples to increase his or her mastery of use of each problem type (Concrete, Semiconcrete, Abstract), ensuring that the student masters each prior to progressing to the next higher level. Vary the medium for acquiring mastery of each problem type, by having students work on the computer, use flashcards, or work in pairs. Pair a struggling student with a peer who has mastered the CSA model and have them jointly apply each step to several mathematics word problems. Debrief with struggling learner, providing opportunity for student to reflect on the problem type (i.e., Concrete, Semiconcrete, Abstract) for different mathematics problems. Provide struggling student with a template to help him or her determine the problem type. Instruct struggling student to develop numerous simple examples of each problem type to develop mastery. Support the teaching of each problem type with visuals and a scaffolding process, demonstrating how to determine the mathematical problem type.

Intervention: *Unitary, Decade, Sequence, Separate, Integrated Model*

Primary Instructional Type	Primary Target Population	Primary Target Content Area(s)
__X__ Direct ____ Cooperative ____ Independent	The primary target population is elementary students who need to master early math skills.	The primary target content areas are early mathematics skills, especially multidigit numbers.

INTERVENTION OVERVIEW ■ The Unitary, Decade, Sequence, Separate, Integrated (UDSSI) model is a five-stage intervention model for helping learners acquire and master multidigit mathematics skills (Fuson et al., 1997). These authors stress the importance of adhering to the stages in their established sequence: *U*nitary, *D*ecade, *S*equence, *S*eparate, and *I*ntegrate. Mathematics skills acquired in each stage provide the foundation for success in the subsequent stages, with a specific emphasis on two-digit conceptual structures.

INSTRUCTIONAL USAGE ■ The UDSSI model is used with any learner in the elementary school grades who is learning early mathematical skills, including struggling students. The UDSSI model helps learners develop various early mathematics skills, including number concepts, counting, sequencing, two-digit inferences (e.g., 35 represents three tens and five ones), and the combination of these skills. Teachers who use this model are better able to identify a student's mathematical strengths and needs in early stages of math development (Bender, 2009).

RESEARCH-BASED EVIDENCE ■ Jones et al. (1996) wrote that use of the UDSSI model assists learners to develop a solid foundation for acquiring multidigit number concepts in the early elementary grades. Fuson and Wearne (1997) indicated that use of the five-stage sequence helps learners improve their understanding of multidigit numbers and more complex mathematics problems.

EXPECTED LEARNER OUTCOME(S) ■ Through use of the UDSSI intervention model, learners acquire a greater understanding of multidigit concepts and skills and increase their skills in solving more complex mathematics problems.

STEPS TO IMPLEMENTATION ■ Implementation of the UDSSI model requires teachers and students to adhere to the following research-based stages, directed by the teacher:

1. *Unitary Stage*—This stage reflects early development and understanding of number representation (e.g., 5 represents five objects or items) and place value for numbers into the teens.

2. *Decade Stage*—This stage engages students in counting by tens. In addition, students master number order and counting higher than 19, with a goal of being able to count from 1 to 99.

3. *Sequence Stage*—This stage emphasizes the further development of the sequence of tens and ones (e.g., students learn that 42 represents four tens and two ones). Students learn that the first number is always written first, followed by the second number. Students in this stage are able to write the numbers properly (e.g., 42 is written 4 and then 2, not 40 and 2).

4. *Separate Stage*—Building on the previous stages, learners become more proficient in separating out numbers and attaching the concept of tens and ones to numbers (e.g., 58 means five tens and eight ones). Separation of the tens and ones becomes more automatic during this stage.

5. *Integrated Stage*—As learners combine the Sequence and Separate stages, they integrate the skills they need to solve multidigit problems. This stage assists learners to understand that the order of one to nine is repeated throughout hundreds, thousands, etc., and they gain the ability to automatically identify and use tens and ones place values in two-digit problems.

As teachers implement the UDSSI model, they incorporate the CSA intervention process. Learners initially rely on concrete objects to solve problems, progress to a more representational level by not needing concrete objects, and finally are able to solve multidigit problems by grouping and regrouping numbers for easy calculation.

IMPLEMENTATION FIDELITY CHECK ■ The UDSSI model is implemented with fidelity when the teacher observes student performance and ensures that students learn the skills in each of the five stages in sequence. In addition, teachers may develop and complete a simple checklist as the learner engages in the mathematics tasks associated with each of the stages.

INTERVENTION EFFECTIVENESS CHECKS ■ The USDDI model is designed to help students master early mathematic abilities.

▶ **Progress-Monitoring Data Collection Device(s):** Use a mathematics probe.

▶ **Frequency of Monitoring Data Collection:** Collect data every 10–15 school days.

▶ **Diagnostic Assessment:** Use individual mathematics tests (e.g., Test of Early Mathematics Ability).

▶ **Lack of Progress (Intervention Adjustments):** Provide struggling learner numerous mathematics examples to increase mastery of each mathematical stage, ensuring mastery of each stage prior to progressing to next higher stage. Vary the medium for acquiring mastery of each stage by having the student work on the computer, use flashcards, work in a pair, etc. Pair struggling student with a peer who has mastered each of the five mathematical stages and have them jointly use each stage to demonstrate mastery. Debrief with struggling learner, providing opportunity for student to reflect on each stage for different mathematics problems. Provide struggling student with a template guiding his or her use of each problem stage. Instruct struggling student to develop numerous simple examples of each mathematical stage to develop mastery. Support the teaching of each mathematical stage with visuals and a scaffolding process, demonstrating effective application of each stage in a sequential and systematic manner.

Intervention: *Cognitive Guided Instruction*

Primary Instructional Type	Primary Target Population	Primary Target Content Area(s)
_X_ Direct ____ Cooperative ____ Independent	The primary target population is learners, including those who struggle with problem solving.	The primary target content areas are simple and complex mathematics problems that use algebra.

INTERVENTION OVERVIEW ■ Cognitive Guided Instruction (CGI) combines cognitive processes, such as visualization, with self-regulation strategies, such as self-questioning (Montague & Dietz, 2009). CGI assists learners to visualize math problems by building on their prior knowledge. The CGI process involves activating prior knowledge, explicit teaching, guided and independent practice, modeling, and scaffolding designed to help learners better understand, analyze, evaluate, and solve mathematical problems by incorporating self-regulated and visualization strategies into the process.

INSTRUCTIONAL USAGE ■ CGI is used to help learners, including struggling learners, to become more efficient at solving mathematical problems. According to Bender (2009), this intervention is best used with groups of students because they are able to share responses and visualizations with one another during the learning process. CGI is effective at guiding learners through the CSA intervention sequence, resulting in more effective abstract problem-solving.

RESEARCH-BASED EVIDENCE ■ CGI helps learners to more effectively visualize mathematical problems (Bender, 2009). Montague and Dietz (2009) wrote that CGI appears to be effective for use with students who are solving strategic learning problems for which they need to use visualization and self-regulated strategies. The National Mathematics Advisory Panel (2008) suggested that CGI, which is a form of constructivist learning, is effective because teachers cannot always transmit mathematical knowledge and skills directly to students. Rather, teachers must guide students in a process that assists learners to develop skills in self-directed and regulated ways.

EXPECTED LEARNER OUTCOME(S) ■ The systematic application of CGI is expected to help students develop more self-directed and self-monitored learning. In addition, through both teacher-directed and peer-mediated instruction, CGI helps students become more efficient at selecting and using effective strategies, while avoiding strategies that are less effective in solving mathematics problems.

STEPS TO IMPLEMENTATION ■ A variety of steps may be used in the overall implementation of cognitive guided instruction (see Behrend, 2003; Bender, 2009; and Montague & Dietz, 2009). Discussions found in Montague (1992) present the following steps to solve a mathematics word problem, completed by student groups with teacher guidance:

Step 1: Read math problem.

Step 2: Paraphrase what the problem is stating in own words.

Step 3: Draw a schematic diagram to visually represent what the problem is asking or requires from the student (i.e., is it a change, group, or comparison problem).

Step 4: Establish a plan to solve the problem, using a self-regulated strategy such as SOLVE IT (see Table 2.2).

Step 5: Estimate or predict correct answer.

Step 6: Complete needed computation to solve problem.

Step 7: Determine whether problem is correctly solved, and self-monitor the effects of the process in producing the correct response.

By guiding students to adhere to a structured process for solving mathematics problems such as the one just illustrated, teachers help learners develop and use visualization and self-regulated strategies, leading to more independent abstract learning. There are other, similar processes for using CGI in the classroom, and the reader is referred to the previously mentioned sources for additional examples.

IMPLEMENTATION FIDELITY CHECK ■ The fidelity of implementation of CGI requires teachers to adhere to established structures, such as the list of steps provided, by periodically checking to make certain that the students are following the required steps. Teachers may use a simple checklist to record when a small group of students completes each step. In addition, debriefing with the students after they have completed a mathematics problem-solving session using CGI allows learners to describe their experiences and inform the teacher of CGI effectiveness at using visualizations and self-regulated learning.

INTERVENTION EFFECTIVENESS CHECKS ■ CGI is designed to improve students' abilities to solve mathematical word problems.

▶ **Progress-Monitoring Data Collection Device(s):**   Use a mathematics probe.

▶ **Frequency of Monitoring Data Collection:**   Collect data every 10–15 school days.

▶ **Diagnostic Assessment:**   Use individual mathematics tests (e.g., Comprehensive Mathematical Abilities Test).

▶ **Lack of Progress (Intervention Adjustments):**   Provide additional support to struggling learner to increase mastery of use of the seven Steps to Implementation of CGI. Pair struggling student with a peer who has mastered the Steps to Implementation of CGI and have them jointly apply the steps to several mathematics word problems to ensure mastery. Debrief with struggling learner, providing opportunity for student to reflect on the word problem and describe how visualization and self-questioning assisted in completion of the mathematical problem (e.g., using techniques such as Estimation, Paraphrasing). Provide struggling student with a template guiding application of each of the CGI steps to solving mathematical problems. Instruct struggling student to complete each of the seven steps, individually, for numerous mathematical word problems, proceeding to the next step only after mastery of the previous step. Support the teaching of the seven steps of CGI with visuals and a scaffolding process, demonstrating effective use in mathematical word problems.

Intervention: *Classwide Peer Tutoring–Mathematics*

Note: The application of CWPT to reading instruction was described in detail in Chapter 4, and the reader is referred to that description for a review of this intervention. Described here are specific uses of CWPT for mathematics.

Primary Instructional Type	Primary Target Population	Primary Target Content Area(s)
____ Direct _X_ Cooperative ____ Independent	The primary target population is students in elementary and middle school grades.	The primary target content areas are any mathematical skills or concepts.

INTERVENTION OVERVIEW ■ See reading example in Chapter 4.

INSTRUCTIONAL USAGE ■ CWPT is effective for teaching most mathematical skills and concepts in situations in which pairs of learners work together in completing math tasks.

RESEARCH-BASED EVIDENCE ■ CWPT in mathematics is particularly effective when it is used during the guided or independent practice stages of instruction (Bender, 2009). Several other researchers have found CWPT-Mathematics to be effective in teaching math skills to students in both the elementary and middle school levels (Allsopp, 1997; Mortweet et al., 1999; National Mathematics Advisory Panel, 2008).

EXPECTED LEARNER OUTCOME(S) ■ Use of CWPT-Mathematics helps students to acquire core mathematics concepts and skills in more motivating and personalized ways by providing greater opportunities for them to learn in a cooperative environment.

STEPS TO IMPLEMENTATION ■ See reading example in Chapter 4.

IMPLEMENTATION FIDELITY CHECK ■ See reading example in Chapter 4.

INTERVENTION EFFECTIVENESS CHECKS ■ CWPT-Mathematics is designed to improve students' overall academic progress in mathematics.

▶ **Progress-Monitoring Data Collection Device(s):** Use mathematics fluency and word problem passage or probe.

▶ **Frequency of Monitoring Data Collection:** Collect data every 10–12 school days.

▶ **Diagnostic Assessment:** Use individual mathematics tests (e.g., Comprehensive Mathematical Abilities Test).

▶ **Lack of Progress (Intervention Adjustments):** Reteach the four CWPT steps. Help struggling student select questions to ask in role of tutor. Provide teacher support to struggling tutee by suggesting strategies for responding to tutor questions. Reinforce the training provided (Step Two) with periodic checks to ensure students are properly implementing CWPT. Strategically place struggling tutor or tutee in a pair with a stronger student to facilitate initial successes.

Intervention: *Peer-Assisted Learning Strategies–Mathematics*

Note: The application of PALS to reading instruction was described in detail in Chapter 4, and the reader is referred to that description for review of this intervention. Described here are specific uses of PALS for mathematics.

Primary Instructional Type	Primary Target Population	Primary Target Content Area(s)
____ Direct __X__ Cooperative ____ Independent	The primary target population is learners in grades K–6.	The primary target content areas are basic mathematics skills and concepts that typically are taught in grades K–6.

INTERVENTION OVERVIEW ▪ PALS–Mathematics supplements Tier 1 core instruction. It includes worksheets and game boards to assist students to acquire and master basic math skills. (To learn more, visit kc.vanderbilt.edu/pals/.)

INSTRUCTIONAL USAGE ▪ PALS–Mathematics is implemented two to three times per week for approximately 30 minutes per session to supplement Tier 1 core mathematics curricula and programs (i.e., it functions as Tier 2 support).

RESEARCH-BASED EVIDENCE ▪ Research results over the past several years show that PALS–Mathematics helps both struggling and nonstruggling learners make greater progress than peers educated without the use of PALS (Council for Exceptional Children website).

EXPECTED LEARNER OUTCOME(S) ▪ Through use of PALS–Mathematics, learners will acquire and maintain basic mathematics skills and concepts taught in grades K–6.

STEPS TO IMPLEMENTATION ▪ See reading example in Chapter 4.

IMPLEMENTATION FIDELITY CHECK ▪ See reading example in Chapter 4.

INTERVENTION EFFECTIVENESS CHECKS ▪ PALS–Mathematics is designed to improve students' basic mathematics skills.

▶ **Progress-Monitoring Data Collection Device(s):** Use mathematics fluency and word problem passage or probe.

▶ **Frequency of Monitoring Data Collection:** Collect data every 10–12 school days.

▶ **Diagnostic Assessment:**   Use individual mathematics tests (e.g., Test of Mathematical Abilities, Test of Early Mathematics Ability).

▶ **Lack of Progress (Intervention Adjustments):**   Provide struggling learner additional training in the four PALS strategies and pair learner with the teacher to demonstrate use of each. Pair struggling learner with a peer and have both assume the same PALS roles until struggling student is able to successfully implement each role individually. Provide struggling learner with some sample questions relevant to the math problems to use as a guide for generating his or her own questions. Assist struggling learner to master each of the four Activity Steps in sequential order. Forego the "competition" aspect of the strategy to increase struggling learners' confidence and success.

Intervention: *MATHFACT Guidelines*

Primary Instructional Type	Primary Target Population	Primary Target Content Area(s)
_X_ Direct ____ Cooperative ____ Independent	The primary target population is learners who are struggling to acquire basic math facts.	The primary target content areas are basic mathematics facts.

INTERVENTION OVERVIEW ■ MATHFACT is a set of 10 guidelines that were developed by Thornton and Toohey (1985) to modify the sequence and presentation of basic math facts to struggling learners.

INSTRUCTIONAL USAGE ■ MATHFACT guidelines form the foundation for a program in which learners are provided modified instruction to meet their individual learner needs (Mercer et al., 2011). The project was developed and used initially in Queensland, Australia.

RESEARCH-BASED EVIDENCE ■ The 10 guidelines that form the basis for the MATHFACT program are grounded in research literature and have been used successfully in the classroom (Mercer et al., 2011).

EXPECTED LEARNER OUTCOME(S) ■ Through use of MATHFACT guidelines and alteration of instruction to meet differing learning needs, learners are expected to become more successful at acquiring basic mathematics facts.

STEPS TO IMPLEMENTATION ■ MATHFACT guidelines are summarized here from discussions in Mercer et al. (2011), and the reader is referred to this source for additional information:

1. Identify and reteach prerequisite skills.

2. Conduct ongoing assessment and diagnosis of students' rates of progress, acquired skills, and basic mathematical errors.

3. Modify sequence for learning math facts to accommodate students' individual learning needs.

4. Teach strategies for solving problems prior to implementing drill and practice (e.g., SBI, Evaluation).

5. Modify how mathematics problems are presented on the basis of learner preference and experiential background (e.g., use of concrete objects, visual illustrations).

6. Adjust pace in learning mathematics concepts on the basis of learner progress.

7. Help students select the most appropriate learning strategy to use for specific types of math problems. (For example, learners might use the SOLVE IT strategy presented in Table 2.2.)

8. Repeat verbal prompts to reinforce learning and to further develop independent learning.

9. Help students develop self-regulation skills such as Evaluation or Active Processing by teaching learners how to learn.

10. Provide sufficient opportunities for students to overlearn math concepts or skills after they have initially acquired the skills.

IMPLEMENTATION FIDELITY CHECK ■ To best facilitate implementation fidelity of the MATHFACT guidelines, teachers should develop a simple checklist and record a check each time the different guidelines are used by the students and reinforced by the teacher through reteaching.

INTERVENTION EFFECTIVENESS CHECKS ■ MATHFACT is a set of guidelines that are designed to improve basic mathematics skills.

▶ **Progress-Monitoring Data Collection Device(s):** Use mathematics fluency and word problem passage or probe.

▶ **Frequency of Monitoring Data Collection:** Collect data every 10–12 school days.

▶ **Diagnostic Assessment:** Use individual mathematics tests (e.g., Test of Mathematical Abilities).

▶ **Lack of Progress (Intervention Adjustments):** Provide additional support to struggling learner by increasing use of the 10 Steps to Implementation of

MATHFACT. Pair a struggling student with a peer who has acquired the basic math facts that the struggling student is trying to learn, and implement the Steps to Implementation to the pair so that the student who has mastered the facts can demonstrate the MATHFACT process to the struggling learner. Debrief with struggling learner, providing opportunity to reflect on how the MATHFACT steps help to acquire math facts. Provide struggling student with a template guiding application of each of the MATHFACT steps to acquiring basic math facts. Support the teaching of basic math facts using the steps in MATHFACTS with visuals and a scaffolding process, demonstrating effective use to struggling students (e.g., visually demonstrate Steps 5, 8 , 9, and 10) to ensure that overlearning of the math facts occurs.

Comprehensive Mathematics Instructional Support Programs

A key strength in using the preceding evidence-based practices is that they may be used with or supplemental to a variety of comprehensive Tier 1 core mathematics curricula that already are in use in the classroom. The practices described require little or no purchasing of separate materials, which makes them highly usable and functional for most classrooms where math needs require additional supports. Although the delivery of comprehensive math programs is the foundation for meeting Tier 1 and 2 instructional needs, there are some additional programs designed to assist students who struggle with math, summarized in Table 6.4. The list of programs, which is not an all-inclusive list, comprises comprehensive programs that include necessary materials, activities, and supports to meet the individual needs of any learner, especially struggling learners, including those with a math disability. These programs may be expensive and therefore may not be available in different schools; their descriptions are provided in order to share the key aspects of the programs. The reader is referred to each program's publisher, provided in parentheses after the program name, for additional information.

Strategies for Differentiated Mathematics Instruction

In addition to comprehensive mathematics core and supplemental curricula and structured EBIs, there exist numerous teacher and student strategies to ensure implementation of a differentiated classroom. A variety of these techniques were previously presented in Tables 2.1 and 2.2, with several being specific to differentiating math instruction. The reader is referred to these tables for a review of those mathematics strategies. Unlike the more highly structured

TABLE 6.4 Comprehensive Mathematics Programs

Program	Brief Description
Connecting Math Concepts Series (*SRA*)	A systematic approach using explicit strategies that teaches students connections between math concepts
Corrective Mathematics (*SRA*)	Remedial program to assist learners from third grade to post-secondary school who struggle with learning basic mathematics operations
Direct Instruction Math (*Merrill*)	Comprehensive program using direct instruction for teaching mathematics
Distar Arithmetic (*McGraw-Hill*)	Direct instruction approach to systematically teaching basic math skills, leading to student mastery in grades K–3
I CAN Learn (*I Can Learn website*)	Interactive web-based full math program that is based on mastery for upper elementary and secondary learners
KeyMath—3 Essential Resources (*Pearson*)	Comprehensive program for meeting individual learning needs
Mastering Math (*Steck Vaughn*)	Supplemental program for learners who require additional practice and supports to the core curriculum
Math Triumphs (*McGraw-Hill*)	Program for use with learners who are two or more years below grade level in mathematics, emphasizing foundational skills and concepts for each grade level (K–8)
Pinpoint Math (*McGraw-Hill*)	Program for supplementing math instruction for struggling learners in grades 1–7
Saxon Math (*Houghton Mifflin Harcourt*)	Highly structured K–12 mathematics program
Strategic Math Series (*Edge Enterprises*)	Process for teaching basic math facts to students who have learning difficulties
Teaching Mathematics Series (*NCTM Website*)	Classroom activities and strategies for teaching mathematics. The program uses separate elementary, middle school, and high school resource books
TransMath (*Sporis West*)	Comprehensive intervention program for students who are performing two or more years below grade level

math EBIs that were previously presented, these various strategies are often simple techniques requiring little prior training that are easily incorporated into any classroom structure, Tier 1 core curriculum, or Tier 2 supplemental supports. The use of differentiated teaching strategies to support mathematics instruction is essential given that many of the recommended instructional adjustments are best implemented within the Tier 1 core curriculum.

Although many teachers already use some of the suggested teaching techniques that have been presented, in Table 6.5 they are again presented to reinforce the importance of their use. They may be used with the other interventions presented in order to provide struggling learners math supports within a comprehensive mathematics curriculum (i.e., Tiers 1 and 2). The

TABLE 6.5 Teaching Strategies for Effective Mathematics Instruction

Strategy	Strategy
Explicit modeling of math strategy usage	Directly teach concepts and rules
Follow concrete-semiconcrete-abstract sequence	Teach towards mastery
Focus on generalization of skills	Scaffold instruction
Maintain interactive dialogue about math	Teach various math learning strategies
Teach sequential steps for solving word problems	Use graphic representation/organizers
Apply student self-monitoring to math tasks	Pair objects with numbers
Develop fun and creative activities	Use manipulatives and computer programs
Encourage use of peer-mediated learning tasks	Teach or color-code cue words and phrases
Embed differentiated strategies into program	Strategically use calculators
Assist students to construct math learning	Employ teacher/student questioning
Encourage student journaling about mathematics	Task-analyze math problems
Teach alternative algorithms to support learning	Develop and teach error analysis skills

strategies in the table are not all-inclusive and the reader is referred to the sources that were used to develop the table for additional information (Bender, 2009; Cohen & Spenciner, 2009; Haager & Klingner, 2005; Mercer, Mercer, & Pullen, 2011; Spangler, 2010).

As shown, numerous easy-to-implement mathematics strategies provide learners with necessary differentiations to prevent their needs from becoming more significant before or after they have been identified through screening or progress monitoring.

Use of these differentiated strategies supports Tier 1 and 2 instruction; the strategies do not replace the need to implement the various mathematics EBIs and models presented in this chapter.

CONCLUSION

Like the other two content areas emphasized in this text, the identification of learning needs through screening and progress monitoring is an initial first step in helping all learners progress with mathematics in the classroom. After needs have been identified, the issue of properly adjusting math instruction emerges, challenging educators to (a) ensure that a differentiated math classroom exists in which teachers and students employ a variety of simple-to-implement differentiation strategies and selected EBIs in Tier 1, (b) make correct decisions concerning the implementation of Tier 2 instruction and requiring proper selection of evidence-based mathematics interventions, or (c) select use of an alternate research-based math curriculum to meet more significant learning needs. The key to these three tasks is sufficiently understanding why and how to use selected differentiated strategies, EBIs, and/or RBCs within the framework of Tiers 1 and 2. By carefully studying the mathematics strategies, curricula, and interventions described in this chapter, educators can become more informed, leading to more effective instructional adjustments that increase progress for all students.

CHAPTER 7

Concluding Remarks: Meeting the Classroom Challenges of Multi-Tiered Instruction

THE SUCCESSFUL IMPLEMENTATION OF multi-tiered instruction is the foundation for the RTI framework, and selecting appropriate interventions is critical to the success of a multi-tiered model. In this chapter we will tie together critical multi-tiered concepts and practices. The figure that follows visually illustrates the key multi-tiered model components presented. Each of these components is essential both to understanding the underpinnings of an RTI framework and to implementing tiered instruction for all learners. Although the content areas emphasized in this text are the core instructional areas of reading, writing, and mathematics, the multi-tiered model is applicable to any content area. It is essential for classroom teachers to implement a multi-tiered model across all content areas with consistency in order for students to achieve long-term success and in order to operationalize the school and district model components.

FIGURE 7.1   Components of Multi-Tiered Instructional Models

The significance of preparing teachers for delivery of a multi-tiered instructional model at the classroom level was emphasized throughout the text, highlighting the need to go beyond district and school-level trainings. The components of a multi-tiered model consider this need as the students and teachers become the primary focus of instructional decision-making, adjustments, teaching intervention selection, and ongoing screening and progress monitoring. Each of the components of multi-tiered instruction within an RTI framework is summarized here to reiterate the significance of its use to meet the needs of all learners, especially those who struggle with reading, writing, or mathematics.

PROPER UNDERLYING STRUCTURES ■ Multi-tiered instruction is essential to successfully implement an RTI model. Tier 1 represents the core general class curriculum that is delivered to all learners. Tier 2 includes instruction that supplements the core instruction for learners who struggle or are at risk for falling behind grade and age-level peers. Tier 3 is intensive instruction provided to learners who demonstrate significant learning needs and require a small group or one-on-one setting, including those with disabilities.

EFFECTIVE IMPLEMENTATION PROCESS ■ After multi-tiered structures are in place, educators are able to effectively and efficiently implement the process of multi-tiered instruction. This implementation includes adhering to a continuum of instructional delivery that (a) begins with an RBC, (b) uses targeted DI for students who struggle, (c) provides supplemental instruction should differentiations fail to help struggling students make adequate progress, and (d) provides intensive interventions to meet more significant learning needs. It is essential that educators provide instruction in the preceding sequence to maintain integrity of multi-tiered models by providing learning supports in an organized manner. The supports progressively increase in duration and intensity to meet the needs identified by screening and progress-monitoring data.

HIGH-QUALITY INSTRUCTION WITH FIDELITY ■ Multi-tiered instructional models within an RTI framework are grounded in the practice of implementing high-quality instruction to make certain that proper instruction exists for all learners before educators consider using more intensive interventions or referring the student for special education. In addition to selecting high-quality instruction and curricula (i.e., an RBC, EBIs, DI), their delivery must be implemented in the manner in which they were researched and validated to reflect proper Tier 1, 2, and 3 instruction.

SCREENING, MONITORING, AND DIAGNOSTIC ASSESSMENTS ■ A multi-tiered instructional model within an RTI framework requires the strategic implementation of three distinct yet related types of assessment. *Universal screening* provides the initial "red flag" that identifies a struggling or at-risk learner. *Progress monitoring* provides educators with quantified data illustrating actual progress relative to RBCs, EBIs, and DI. *Diagnostic assessment* is used to further pinpoint learner needs that surface through screening and monitoring and includes an assessment component within a comprehensive special education eligibility process. It is important to make certain that each of these assessment types is used for purposes and decision-making that reflect what each assessment is designed to measure. For example, data scores from a screening device should be used to screen learners who may be struggling, not to diagnose or place students. Monitoring is for tracking progress, not for screening. The results of diagnostic assessment, in combination with screening and monitoring results, are for pinpointing academic skills to further clarify a potential learning need. Success with multi-tiered instructional models requires that data scores from each assessment type be used as designed and that their importance not be overextended.

INTERVENTION SELECTION ■ The central theme of this text is to assist educators to make the informed decisions necessary to link assessment with appropriate interventions. As discussed in the previous chapters, skipping the application of structured reading, writing, and mathematics interventions by moving too quickly to the use of an alternate curriculum should be avoided to best implement a multi-tiered model with integrity. Educators are encouraged to apply and maintain the evidence-based practice continuum, in proper sequence, of (a) RBC, (b) targeted DI, (c) EBIs, (d) and finally alternate research-based curriculum (A-RBC). Only by adhering to this process is it possible to identify and address reading, writing, and mathematics learning needs in a preventative manner within a multi-tiered model.

CONTINUOUS ASSESSMENT AND DECISION-MAKING ■ After all the preceding components are in place, a multi-tiered instructional model still requires continuous measurement of learners' academic progress. Educators must make timely instructional adjustments to address learning needs quickly. Linking assessment to instruction is grounded in the premise that the best teaching and learning occurs within the context of continuous examination of learner progress relative to instruction, followed by effective use of teaching and behavior management techniques and EBIs.

Principles to Implement a Classroom Multi-Tiered Model Effectively

This text concludes with a listing of several guiding principles that support the effective implementation of a multi-tiered instructional model in today's classrooms:

Guiding Principle 1: Make certain that the proper multi-tiered underlying structures are in place for reading, writing, and mathematics instruction.

Guiding Principle 2: Become knowledgeable about the process for effectively delivering instruction in the correct sequence to make certain each of the four types of evidence-based practice is properly implemented (i.e., RBC, DI, EBIs, A-RBC).

Guiding Principle 3: Understand that use of DI by itself is not sufficient to provide Tier 2 supplemental supports.

Guiding Principle 4: Implement EBIs prior to using an A-RBC for most struggling learners.

Guiding Principle 5: Make certain that the RBC is properly implemented (i.e., with fidelity) prior to considering Tier 2 or 3 instruction.

Guiding Principle 6: Link universal screening data scores to selection and implementation of targeted DI in the general classroom prior to using more intensive Tier 2 resources and instruction for most learners.

Guiding Principle 7: Become proficient in screening and progress monitoring utilizing curriculum-based measurement tools (e.g., AIMSweb).

Guiding Principle 8: Structure classroom and instructional management to easily and seamlessly meet diverse needs that students bring to the teaching and learning environment.

Guiding Principle 9: Acquire expertise in the ability to select appropriate interventions using assessment data by initially clarifying the most effective instructional type (i.e., direct, cooperative, independent) to best meet the needs of struggling learners.

Guiding Principle 10: Identify and implement collaboration to best deliver multi-tiered instruction.

Guiding Principle 11: Determine proficiency level, rate of progress, and gap analysis for struggling learners prior to implementing and monitoring instructional adjustments.

Guiding Principle 12: Examine the four key classroom and instructional elements (i.e., Content, Interventions, Instructional Arrangement, Class/ Instructional Management) and assessment data to select the most appropriate intervention to meet Tier 2 needs for struggling learners.

Guiding Principle 13: Acquire expertise in each aspect of evidence-based assessment (see Table 1.2).

Guiding Principle 14: Make certain to implement each aspect of evidence-based practice (i.e., RBC, EBIs, DI) with fidelity and become effective at demonstrating instructional fidelity to colleagues.

Guiding Principle 15: Self-examine own ability to understand, implement, and evaluate changes necessary to successfully implement a multi-tiered instructional model within an RTI framework.

In conclusion, classroom challenges in multi-tiered models are best met as links are made among universal screening, progress monitoring, and diagnostic scores with appropriate EBIs to meet needs in Tier 1, 2, or 3 instruction in the content areas of reading, writing, and mathematics.

References

CHAPTER 1

Bender, W. N., & Shores, C. (2007). *Response to intervention: A practical guide for every teacher*. Thousand Oaks, CA: Corwin Press.

Fuchs, D., & Fuchs, L. S. (2006). Introduction to response to intervention: What, why, and how valid is it? *Reading Research Quarterly, 41* (1), 95–99.

Haager, D., Klingner, J., & Vaughn, S. (2007). *Evidence-based reading practices for response to intervention*. Baltimore: Brookes Publishing.

Hoover, J. J. (2012). Reducing unnecessary referrals of ELLs in RTI: *Assessment, instruction, decision making*. Workshop presentation to the New York City Board of Education, New York, NY, February.

Hoover, J. J. (2011a). Making informed instructional adjustments in RTI models: Essentials for practitioners. *Intervention in School and Clinic 47*(2), 82–90.

Hoover, J. J. (2011b). *Response to intervention models: Curricular implications and interventions*. Upper Saddle River, NJ: Allyn & Bacon/Pearson.

Hoover, J. J. (2010). Special education eligibility decision making in response to intervention models. In J. Klingner & M. J. Orosco (Eds.), *Response to intervention: Critical issues. Theory into Practice, 49*(4), 289–296.

Hoover, J. J. (2009a). *RTI assessment essentials for struggling learners*. Thousand Oaks, CA: Corwin.

Hoover, J. J. (2009b). *Differentiating learning differences from disabilities: Meeting diverse needs through multi-tiered response to intervention*. Upper Saddle River, NJ: Pearson/Allyn & Bacon.

Hoover, J. J., & Love, E. (2011). Supporting school-based response to intervention: A practitioner's model. *Teaching Exceptional Children*, Jan/Feb, 40–48.

Mellard, D. F., & Johnson, E. (2008). *RTI: A practitioner's guide to implementing response to intervention*. Thousand Oaks, CA: Corwin Press.

Moran, D. J., & Malott, R. W. (2004). *Evidence-based educational methods*. Boston: Elsevier Academic Press.

National Association of State Directors of Special Education, Inc. (2005). *Response to intervention: Policy considerations and implementation*. Alexandria, VA: Author.

Tomlinson, C. A. (2001). *How to differentiate instruction in mixed-ability classrooms* (2nd ed.). Alexandria, VA: Association for Supervision and Curriculum Development.

Vaughn, S. (2003). *How many tiers are needed for response to intervention to achieve Acceptable prevention outcomes?* Paper presented at the National Center on Learning Disabilities Responsiveness-to-Interventions Symposium, Kansas City, MO. December, 2003.

Yell, M. (2004, February). *Understanding the three-tier model*. Presentation at the Colorado State Directors of Special Education Meeting, Denver, CO.

CHAPTER 2

AIMSweb. Retrieved September 10, 2010, from aimsweb.com.

Bender, W. N., & Shores, C. (2007). *Response to intervention: A practical guide for every teacher*. Thousand Oaks, CA: Corwin Press.

Boss, C., & Vaughn, S. (2006). *Strategies for Teaching Students with Learning and Behavior Problems*. Boston, MA: Allyn & Bacon.

Burns, M. K., & Gibbons, K. A. (2008). *Implementing response-to-intervention in elementary and secondary schools: Procedures to assure scientific-based practices*. New York: Taylor & Francis.

Colorado Department of Education (2008). *Response to intervention (RtI): A practitioner's guide to implementation*. Denver, CO: Colorado Department of Education.

Council for Exceptional Children. (2007). *Peer Assisted Learning Strategies*. Retrieved November 12, 2010, from www.cec.sped.org.

Czarnecki, E., Rosko, D., & Pine, E. (1998). How to call up note-taking skills. *Teaching Exceptional Children, 30*, 14–19.

De la Paz, S. (1997). Strategy instruction in planning: Teaching students with learning and writing disabilities to compose persuasive and expository essays. *Learning Disability Quarterly, 20*, 227–248.

Deno, S. L. (1985). Curriculum-based measurement: The emerging alternative. *Exceptional Children, 52*, 219–232.

Deno, S. L. (2005[HS2]). Problem-solving assessment. In R. Brown-Chidsey (Ed.), *Assessment for intervention: A problem-solving approach* (pp. 10–40). New York: Guilford Press.

Fuchs, D., & Fuchs, L. S. (2007). The role of assessment in the three-tier approach to reading instruction. In D. Haager, J. Klingner, & S. Vaughn (Eds.), *Evidence-based reading practices for response to intervention* (pp. 29–42). Baltimore: Brookes Publishing.

Fuchs, D., & Fuchs, L. S. (2006). Introduction to response to intervention: What, why, and how valid is it? *Reading Research Quarterly, 41* (1), 95–99.

Fuchs, D., & Fuchs, L. S. (1998). Treatment validity: A unifying concept for reconceptualizing the identification of learning disabilities. *Learning Disabilities Research & Practice, 13*, 204–219.

Hoover, J. J. (2011a). Making informed instructional adjustments in RTI models: Essentials for practitioners. *Intervention in School and Clinic, 47*(2), 82–90.

Hoover, J. J. (2011b). *Response to intervention models: Curricular implications and interventions.* Upper Saddle River, NJ: Allyn & Bacon/Pearson.

Hoover, J. J., & Patton, J. R. (2007). *Teaching study skills to students with learning problems: A teacher's guide to meeting diverse needs.* Austin, TX: Pro-Ed.

Hoover, J. J., & Patton, J. R. (2005). *Curriculum adaptations for students with learning and behavior problems* (3rd ed.). Austin, TX: Pro-Ed.

Hosp, M. K., Hosp, J. L., & Howell, K. W. (2007). *The ABCs of CBM: A practical guide to curriculum-based measurement.* New York: Guilford Press.

IDEA. (2004). *Individuals with Disabilities Education Act Amendments of 2004,* Washington, DC.

Meese, R. L. (2001). *Teaching learners with mild disabilities: Integrating research and practice* (2nd ed.). Belmont, CA: Wadsworth/Thompson Learning.

Mellard, D. F., & Johnson, E. (2008). *RTI: A practitioner's guide to implementing response to intervention.* Thousand Oaks, CA: Corwin Press.

Ogle. D. (1996). A teaching model that develops active reading of expository text. *The Reading Teacher, 39,* 564–570.

Shapiro, E. S. (2008). Best practices in setting progress monitoring goals for academic skill improvement. In A. Thomas & J. Grimes (Eds.), *Best practices in school psychology V* (pp. 141–157). Bethesda, MD: National Association of School Psychologists.

Shinn, M. R., & Shinn, M. M. (2002). *AIMSweb training workbook: Administration and scoring of reading curriculum-based measurement (R-CBM) for use in general outcome measurement.* Eden Prairie, MN: Edformation, Inc. Retrieved September 15, 2010, from aimsweb.com.

Sprenger, M. B. (2008). *Differentiation through learning styles and memory* (2nd ed.). Thousand Oaks, CA: Corwin Press.

Stecker, P. M., & Lembke, E. S. (2005). *Advanced applications of CBM in reading: Instructional decision-making strategies manual.* Washington, DC: National Center on Student Progress Monitoring.

Tomlinson, C. A. (2001). *How to differentiate instruction in mixed-ability classrooms* (2nd ed.). Alexandria, VA: Association for Supervision and Curriculum Development.

CHAPTER 3

Batsche, G. M., Curtis, M. J., Dorman, C., Castillo, J. M., & Porter, L. J. (2007). The Florida problem solving/response to intervention model: Implementing a statewide initiative. In S. R. Jimerson, M. K. Burns, & A. M. VanDerHeyden (Eds.), *Handbook of response to intervention: The science and practice of assessment and intervention* (pp. 378–395). New York: Springer.

Fixsen, D., Naoom, S., Blasé, K., & Wallace, F. (2007, Winter/Spring). Implementation: The missing link between research and practice. *The APSAC Advisor,* 4–10.

Hall, S. L. (2008). *A principal's guide: Implementing response to intervention.* Thousand Oaks, CA: Corwin Press.

Hoover, J. J. (2011b). *Response to intervention models: Curricular implications and interventions.* Upper Saddle River, NJ: Allyn & Bacon/Pearson.

Hoover, J. J., & Patton, J. R. (2008). The role of special educators in a multi-tiered instructional system. *Intervention in School and Clinic, 43,* 195–202.

Hoover, J. J., & Patton, J. R. (2005). *Curriculum adaptations for students with learning and behavior problems* (3rd ed.). Austin, TX: Pro-Ed.

Idol, L. (2002). *Creating collaborative and inclusive schools.* Evergreen, CO: Lorna Idol.

Johnson, E. S., Carter, D. R., & Pool, J. (2010) *Implementing a Combined RTI/PBS Model: Getting Started.* RTI Action Network. Retrieved October 19, 2011, from www.rtinetwork.org.

Walther-Thomas, C., Korinek, L., & McLaughlin, V. L. (2005). Collaboration to support student's success. In T. M. Skrtic, K. R. Harris, & J. G. Shriner (eds.). *Special education policy and practice: Accountability, instruction and social challenges* (pp. 182–211). Denver, CO: Love Publishing.

Weiner, H. M. (2003). Effective inclusion: Professional development in the context of the classroom. *Teaching Exceptional Children, 35*(6), 12–18.

CHAPTER 4

Allen, R. V. (1976). *Language experiences in communication.* Boston: Houghton Mifflin.

Arreaga-Mayer, C. (1998). Increasing active student responding and improving academic performance through classwide peer tutoring. *Intervention in School and Clinic, 34,* 89–94.

Ashton-Warner, S. (1963). *Teacher.* New York: Bantam Books.

Bos, C. S. (1991). Reading–writing connections: Using literature as a zone of proximal development for writing. *Learning Disabilities Research & Practice, 6,* 251–256.

Bos, C. S., & Anders, P. L. (1992). Using interactive teaching and learning strategies to promote text comprehension and content learning for students with learning disabilities. *International Journal of Disability, Development and Education, 39,* 225–238.

Chapman, C., & King, R. (2003). *Differentiated instructional strategies for reading in the content areas.* Thousand Oaks, CA: Sage.

Clay, M. M. (1993). *Reading recovery: A guidebook for teachers in training.* Portsmouth, NH: Heinemann.

Clay, M. M. (1985). *The early detection of reading difficulties* (3rd ed.). Auckland, New Zealand: Heinemann Educational Books.

Cote, N., & Goldman, S. R. (1999). Building representations of informational text: Evidence from children's think-aloud protocols. In H. van Oostendorp & S. R. Goldman, *The construction of mental representations during reading* (pp. 169–193). Mahwah, NJ: Erlbaum.

D'Agostino, J. V., & Murphy, J. A. (2004). A meta-analysis of Reading Recovery in United States schools. *Educational Evaluation and Policy Analysis, 26,* 23–38.

De la Colina, M. G., Parker, R. I., Hasbrouck, J. E., & Alecio, R. (2001). An intensive intervention for at-risk bilingual readers. *Bilingual Research Journal. 225*(4), 503–538.

Edmark Associates. *Edmark Reading Program: Teacher's Guide* (1972). Seattle: Author.

Ehri, L. C. (2006). More about phonics: Findings and reflections. In K. A. D. Stahl & M. C. McKenna (Eds.), *Reading research at* word: *Foundations of effective practice* (pp. 155– 165). New York: Guilford Press.

Engelmann, S., & Bruner, E. C. (2002). *Reading mastery*. DeSoto, TX: SRA.

Engelmann, S., Engelmann, O., & Davis, K. L. S. (1998). *Horizons: Learning to read*. Blacklick, OH: SRA.

Englemann, S., Johnson, G., & Carnine, L. (1999). *Corrective reading: Decoding*. Blacklick, OH: SRA.

Fernald, G. (1988). *Remedial techniques in basic school subjects*. Austin, TX: Pro-Ed.

Flood, J., & Lapp, D. (1988). A reader response approach to the teaching of literature. *Reading Research and Instruction, 27*, 61–66.

Gersten, R. M., & Jimenez, R. T. (1994). A delicate balance: Enhancing literature instruction for students of English as a second language. *The Reading Teacher, 47*, 438–449.

Greenwood, C. R., Arreaga-Mayer, C., Utley, C. A., Gavin, K. M., & Terry, B. J. (2001). Class Wide Peer Tutoring Learning Management system: Applications with elementary-level English language learners. *Remedial and Special Education, 22*, 34–47.

Haager, D., & Klingner, J. K. (2005). *Differentiating instruction in inclusive classrooms: The special educator's guide*. Upper Saddle River, NJ: Allyn & Bacon/Pearson.

Harris, A. J., & Sipay, E. R. (1990). *How to increase reading ability: A guide to developmental and remedial methods*. White Plains, NY: Longman.

Hasbrouck, J. E., Ihnot, C., & Rogers, G. (1999). "Read Naturally": A strategy to increase oral reading fluency. *Reading Research and Instruction, 39*(1), 27–38.

Hoover, J. J., Klingner, J., Baca, L. M., & Patton, J. M. (2008). *Methods for teaching culturally and linguistically diverse exceptional learners*. Upper Saddle River, NJ: Merrill/Pearson.

Institute of Education Sciences. (2008). *What Works Clearinghouse intervention report: Reading Recovery*. Washington, DC: U.S. Department of Education.

Joseph, L. M. (2006). Incremental rehearsal: A flashcard drill technique for increasing retention of reading words. *The Reading Teacher, 59*(8), 803–806.

Kim, A., Vaughn, S., Wanzek, J., & Wei, S. (2004). Graphic organizers and their effects on the reading comprehension of students with LD: A synthesis of research. *Journal of Learning Disabilities, 37*(2), 105–118.

Klingner, J. K., & Geisler, D. (2008). Helping classroom reading teachers distinguish between language acquisition and learning disabilities. In J. K. Klingner, J. J. Hoover, & L. M. Baca (Eds.), *Why do English Language Learners struggle with reading: Distinguishing language acquisition for learning disabilities* (pp. 57–73). Thousand Oaks, CA: Corwin Press.

Klingner, J. K., & Vaughn, S. (2000). The helping behaviors of fifth-graders while using collaborative strategic reading (CSR) during ESL content classes. *TESOL Quarterly, 34*, 69–98.

Klingner, J. K., & Vaughn, S. (1999). Promoting reading comprehension, content learning, and English acquisition through collaborative strategic reading (CSR). *The Reading Teacher, 52*, 738–747.

Klingner, J. K., & Vaughn, S. (1996). Reciprocal teaching of reading comprehension strategies for students with learning disabili-

ties who use English as a second language. *Elementary School Journal, 96*, 275–293.

Klingner, J. K., Vaughn, S., Arguelles, M. E., Hughes, M. T., & Ahwee, S. (2004). Collaborative strategic reading: "Real world" lessons from classroom teachers. *Remedial and Special Education, 25*, 291–302.

Klingner, J. K., Vaughn, S., Dimino, J., Schumm, J. S., & Bryant, D. P. (2001). *From clunk to click: Collaborative strategic reading*. Longmont, CO: Sopris West.

MacQuarrie, L. L., Tucker, J. A., Burns, M. K., & Hartman, B. (2002). Comparison of retention rates using traditional, drill sandwich, and incremental rehearsal flash card methods. *School Psychology Review, 31*, 584–595.

McLeskley, J., Rosenberg, M. S., & Westling, D. L. (2010). *Inclusion: Effective practices for all students*. Upper Saddle River, NJ: Merrill/Pearson.

Mercer, C. D., Mercer, A. R., & Pullen, P. C. (2011). *Teaching students with learning and behavior problems*. Upper Saddle River, NJ: Merrill/Pearson.

National Reading Panel. (2000). *Teaching children to read: An evidence-based assessment of the scientific research literature on reading and its implications for reading instruction: summary report*. Washington, DC: National Institute of Child Health and Development.

Palinscar, A. S., & Brown, A. L. (1989). Instruction for self-regulated reading. In L. Resnick & L. Kloepfer (Eds.), *Toward the thinking curriculum: Current cognitive research* (pp. 29–49). Alexandria, VA: Association for Supervision and Curriculum Development.

Palincsar, A. S., & Brown, A. L. (1984). The reciprocal teaching of comprehension–fostering and comprehension-monitoring activities. *Cognition and Instruction, 1*, 117–175.

Palincsar, A. S., & David, Y. M. (1991). Promoting literacy through classroom dialogue. In E. H. Hiebert (Ed.), *Literacy for a diverse society: Perspectives, practices and policies* (pp. 122–139). New York: Teachers College Press.

Peregoy, S. F., & Boyle, O. F. (2001). *Reading, writing, and learning in ESL: A resource book for K–12 teachers* (3rd ed.). New York: Addison Wesley Longman.

Pinnell, G. S. (1990). Success for low achievers through Reading Recovery. *Educational Leadership, 48*(1), 17–21.

Quigley, S., McAnally, P., King, C., & Rose, S. (2001). *Reading milestones*. Austin, TX: Pro-Ed.

Rasinski, T. V., & Hoffman, J. V. (2003). Oral reading in the school literacy curriculum. *Reading Research Quarterly, 38*, 510–523.

Read Naturally. Retrieved from: http://www.readnaturally.com/. September 15, 2011.

Reutzel, D. R., Camperell, K., & Smith, J. A. (2002). Hitting the wall: Helping struggling readers comprehend. In C. C. Block, L. B. Gambrell, & M. Pressley (Eds.), *Improving comprehension instruction: Rethinking research, theory, and classroom practice* (pp. 321–353). San Francisco: John Wiley & Sons.

Richard-Amato, P. A. (1996). *Making it happen: Interaction in the second language classroom*. White Plains, NY: Longman.

Roberts, M. L., & Shapiro, E. S. (1996). Effects of instructional ratios on students' reading performance in a regular education program. *Journal of School Psychology, 34*, 73–91.

Rosenshine, B., & Meister, C. (1994). Reciprocal teaching: A review of the research. *Review of Educational Research, 64,* 479–530.

Short, K. G., and Klassen, C. (1993). Literature circles: Hearing children's voices. In B. E. Cullinan (Ed.), *Children's voices: Talk in the classroom* (pp. 66–85). Newark, DE: International Reading Association.

Skinner, C. H. (2002). An empirical analysis of interspersal research evidence, implications, and applications of the discrete task completion hypothesis. *Journal of School Psychology, 40,* 347–368.

Stahl, S. A., & Miller, P. D. (2006). Whole language and language experience approaches for beginning reading: A quantitative research synthesis. In K. A. D. Stahl & M. C. McKenna (Eds.), *Reading research at work: Foundations of effective practice.* New York: Guilford Press.

Sulzby, E., & Barnhart, J. (1992). The development of academic competence: All our children emerge as writers and readers. In J. W. Irwin & M. A. Doyle (Eds.), *Reading/writing connections: Learning from research* (pp. 120–144). Newark, DE: International Reading Association.

Trainin, G., & Andrzejczak, N. (2006). *Readers' Theatre: A viable reading strategy?* Lincoln, NE: Great Plains Institute of Reading and Writing.

Tucker, J. A. (1989). *Basic flashcard technique when vocabulary is the goal.* Unpublished teaching materials. School of Education, University of Chattanooga. Chattanooga, TN: Author.

Vygotsky, L. S. (1978). *Mind in society.* Cambridge, MA: Harvard University Press.

Wong, B. Y. L., & Jones, W. (1982). Increasing metacomprehension in learning disabled and normally achieving students through self-questioning training. *Learning Disability Quarterly, 5,* 228–240.

CHAPTER 5

Bender, W. N. (2009). *Differentiating math instruction: Strategies that work for K–8 classrooms.* Thousand Oaks, CA: Sage.

Chapman, C., & King, R. (2003). *Differentiated instructional strategies for reading in the content areas.* Thousand Oaks, CA: Sage.

Calkins, L., Hartman, A., & White, Z. (2005). *One to one: The art of conferring with young writers.* Portsmouth, NH: Heinemann.

Collins, J. J. (1997). *Selecting and teaching Focus Concentration Areas: A planning guide.* Rowley, MA: The Network, Inc.

Deshler, D. D., Ellis, E. S., & Lenz, B. K. (1996). *Teaching adolescents with learning disabilities: Strategies and methods* (2nd ed.). Denver, CO: Love.

Echevarria, J., & Graves, A. (2007). *Sheltered content instruction: Teaching students with diverse needs* (3rd ed.). Upper Saddle River, NJ: Allyn & Bacon/Pearson.

Gere, A., & Abbott, R. D. (1985). Talking about writing: The language of writing groups. *Research in the Teaching of English, 19,* 362–385.

Graham, S. (1997). Executive control in the revising of students with learning and writing difficulties. *Journal of Educational Psychology, 89,* 223–234.

Graham, S., & Harris, K. R. (2005). Improving writing performance of young struggling writers: Theoretical and programmatic research from the Center on Accelerating Student Learning. *The Journal of Special Education, 39,* 19–33.

Graham, S., & Harris, K. R. (2002). Prevention and intervention for struggling writers. In M. Shinn, H. Walker, & G. Stoner (Eds.), *Interventions for academic and behavior problems II: Preventive and remedial techniques* (pp. 589–610). Washington, DC: The National Association of School Psychologists.

Graham, S., MacArthur, C. A., & Fitzgerald, J. (2007). *Best practices in writing instruction.* New York: Guilford Press.

Graham, S., & Perin, D. (2006). *Writing next: Effective strategies to improve writing of adolescents in middle and high school.* Washington, DC: Alliance for Excellence in Education.

Graves, A. W. (2008). Teaching written expression to culturally and linguistically diverse exceptional learners. In J. J. Hoover, J. K. Klingner, L. Baca, & J. M. Patton (Eds.), *Methods for teaching culturally and linguistically diverse exceptional learners* (pp. 218–247). Upper Saddle River, NJ: Merrill/Pearson.

Harris, K. R., & Graham, S. (1996). *Making the writing process work: Strategies for composition and self-regulation.* Cambridge, MA: Brookline Books.

Harris, K. R., Graham, S., Mason, L. H., & Friedlander, B. (2008). *Powerful writing strategies for all students.* Baltimore: Brookes Publishing.

Hoover, J. J. (2011a). Making informed instructional adjustments in RTI models: Essentials for practitioners. *Intervention in School and Clinic. 47*(2), 82–90.

Hoover, J. J. (2011b). *Response to intervention models: Curricular implications and interventions.* Upper Saddle River, NJ: Allyn & Bacon/Pearson.

Kansas University Center for Research on Learning. Retrieved November 18, 2011, from www.kucrl.org.

MacArthur, C. A., Graham, S., & Fitzgerald, J. (2006). *Handbook of writing research.* New York: Guilford Press.

MacArthur, C. A., Schwartz, S. S., & Graham, S. (1991). A model for writing instruction: Integrating word processing and strategy instruction into a process approach to writing. *Learning Disabilities Research and Practice, 6,* 230–236.

MacArthur, C., Schwartz, S., Graham, S., Molloy, D., & Harris, K. R. (1996). Integration of strategy instruction into a whole language classroom: A case study. *Learning Disabilities Research & Practice, 11,* 168–176.

Mercer, C. D., Mercer, A. R., & Pullen, P. C. (2011). *Teaching students with learning and behavior problems.* Upper Saddle River, NJ: Merrill/Pearson.

Nixon, J., & Topping, K. (2001). Emergent writing: The impact of structured peer interaction. *Educational Psychology, 21,* 41–58.

Pritchard, R. J., & Honeycutt, R. L. (2007). Best practices in implementing a process approach to teaching writing. In S. Graham, C. A. MacArthur, and J. Fitzgerald (Eds.). *Best practices in writing instruction.* New York: Guilford Press.

Pritchard, R. J., & Honeycutt, R. L. (2006). The process approach to teaching writing: Examining its effectiveness. In C. A. MacArthur, S. Graham, & J. Fitzgerald (Eds.), *Handbook of writing research* (pp. 275–290). New York: Guilford Press.

Tompkins, G. E. (2008). *Teaching writing: Balancing process and product* (5th ed.). Upper Saddle River, NJ: Merrill/Pearson.

Troia, G. A. (2006). Writing instruction for students with learning disabilities. In C. A. MacArthur, S. Graham, & J. Fitzgerald (Eds.), *Handbook of writing research* (pp. 324–336). New York, NY: Guilford.

Zimmerman, B. J., & Risemberg, R. (1997). Becoming a self-regulated writer: A social-cognitive perspective. *Journal of Contemporary Educational Psychology, 22*(1), 70–101.

CHAPTER 6

Allsopp, D. H. (1997). Using classwide peer tutoring to teach beginning algebra problem-solving skills in heterogeneous classrooms. *Remedial and Special Education, 18*(6), 367–379.

Behrend, J. (2003). Learning-disabled students make sense of mathematics. *Teaching Children Mathematics, 9*(5), 269–274.

Bender, W. N. (2009). *Differentiating math instruction: Strategies that work for K–8 classrooms.* Thousand Oaks, CA: Sage.

Bruner, J. (1996). *The Culture of Education.* Cambridge, MA: Harvard University Press.

Cohen, L. G., & Spenciner, L. J. (2009). *Teaching students with mild and moderate disabilities: Research-based practices* (2nd ed.). Upper Saddle River, NJ: Merrill/Pearson.

Fuson, K. C., & Wearne, D. (1997). Children's conceptual structures for multidigit numbers and methods of multidigit addition and subtraction. *Journal of Research in Mathematics Education, 28*(2), 130–163.

Haager, D., & Klingner, J. K. (2005). *Differentiating instruction in inclusive classrooms: The special educator's guide.* Upper Saddle River, NJ: Allyn & Bacon/Pearson.

Jitendra, A. K. (2008). Using schema-based instruction to make appropriate sense of word problems. *Perspectives on Language and Literacy*, Spring, 20–24.

Jones, G. A., Thornton, C.A., Putt, I. J., Hill, K. M., Mogill, A. T., Rich, B.S., & Van Zoest, L. R. (1996). Multidigit number sense: A framework for instruction and assessment. *Journal for Research in Mathematics Education*, 27 (3), 310–336.

Maccini, P., & Gagnon, J. C. (2002). Perceptions and applications of NCTM standards by special and general education teachers. *Exceptional Children, 68*(3), 325–344.

Mercer, C. D., Mercer, A. R., & Pullen, P. C. (2011). *Teaching students with learning and behavior problems.* Upper Saddle River, NJ: Merrill/Pearson.

Miller, S., & Hudson, P. J. (2007). Using evidence-based practices to build mathematics competence related to conceptual, procedural, and declarative knowledge. *Learning Disabilities Research and Practice, 22*(1), 47–57.

Montague, M. (1992). The effects of cognitive and metacognitive strategy instruction on the mathematical problem solving of middle school students with learning disabilities. *Journal of Learning Disabilities, 25*, 230–248.

Montague, M., & Dietz, S. (2009). Evaluating the evidence base for cognitive strategy instruction and mathematical problem solving. *Exceptional Children, 75*(3), 285–302.

Mortweet, S. L., Utley, C. A., Walker, D., Dawson, H. L., Delquadri, J. C., & Reddy, S. S. (1999). Classwide peer tutoring: Teaching students with mild mental retardation in inclusive classrooms. *Exceptional Children, 65*(4), 524–536.

National Council of Teachers of Mathematics. (2000). *Principles and standards for school mathematics.* Reston, VA: Author.

National Mathematics Advisory Panel. (2008). *Foundations for success: The final report of the National Mathematics Advisory Panel.* Washington, DC: U.S. Department of Education.

Peer-Assisted Learning Strategies. Retrieved December 10, 2010, from kc.vanderbilt.edu/pals/.

Seethaler, P. M., & Fuchs, L. S. (2006). The cognitive correlates of computational estimation skill among third-grade students. *Learning Disabilities Research and Practice, 21*, 233–243.

Spangler, D. B. (2010). *Strategies for teaching whole number computation: Using error analysis for intervention and assessment.* Thousand Oaks, CA: Corwin.

Thornton, C. A., & Toohey, M. A. (1985). Basic math facts: Guidelines for teaching and learning. *Learning Disabilities Focus, 1*, 44–57.

Woodward, J. (2006). Developing automaticity in multiplication facts: Integrating strategy instruction with timed practice drills. *Learning Disability Quarterly, 29*(4), 269–290.

Xin, Y. P., Jitendra, K., & Deatline-Buchman, A. (2005). Effects of mathematical word problem solving instruction on students with learning problems. *Journal of Special Education, 39*, 181–192.

Author Index

Subject Index

Contents, as curricular element, 34, 35, 36–37

Continuous evaluation, as component of team collaboration, 53–54

Cooperative-based instruction, 39–40

COPS, study strategy, 24, 135

Corrective Mathematics, comprehensive mathematics programs, 159

Corrective Reading Program, research-based reading program, 105

Council for Exceptional Children, 30

CSA sequence. *See* Concrete-Semiconcrete-Abstract (CSA) sequence

CSR. *See* Collaborative Strategic Reading (CSR)

Curriculum
components, 34–35
delivery of, multi-tiered model and, 20–21
implementation/assessment, 11
research-based (*See* Research-based curriculum (RBC))

Curriculum-based measurement (CBM), 41–43
qualities of, 42
standard directions for one-minute administration, 44

Cut scores, 31

D

Data-based decision maker, educators as, 56, 57

Data scores. *See* Achievement data scores, interpretation of

Decision making
shared, 53

DEFENDS, study strategy, 24, 135

DI. *See* Differentiated instruction (DI)

Diagnose Cards, and CDO Revising Strategy, 124, 125

Diagnostic assessment, 10, 11, 164
Active Processing: Writing, 133
CDO Revising Strategy, 125
CGI, 153
CSA sequence, 148
CSR, 89
CWPT, mathematics intervention, 154
CWPT, reading intervention, 74
Evaluation Strategy: Writing, 131
FCA, 120
Fernald Multisensory Method, 95
Graphic Organizers, 86
Incremental Rehearsal, 104
LEA, 77
LRGs, 84
MATHFACT, 157
PALS, 93
Peer Revising Strategy, 128
Reader's Theater, 99

Reading Recovery, 101

Reading Response Journals, 81

Read Naturally Strategy, 79

Reciprocal Teaching, 71

Report-Writing Strategy, 123
role, in multi-tiered assessment process, 30
SBI, 146
Self-Questioning, 97
SRSD model, 118
UDSSI model, 150

Dialogue questioning
and Reciprocal Teaching, 70–71

Differentiated instruction (DI), 5
as component of evidence-based practice, 9
educators and, 58
mathematics (*See* Differentiating mathematics instruction)
study strategies, 24–27
teaching and student strategies for, 104, 106
teaching/behavior management techniques, 22–23
writing (*See* Differentiating writing instruction)

Differentiating mathematics instruction
strategies for, 158–60

Differentiating writing instruction
strategies for, 134–35

Differentiation Quick Screen (DQS), 35, 46–48

Direct instruction, 39

Direct Instruction Math, comprehensive mathematics programs, 159

Distar Arithmetic, comprehensive mathematics programs, 159

DQS. *See* Differentiation Quick Screen (DQS)

Dual discrepancy, 32

E

EASY, study strategy, 24

EBIs. *See* Evidence-based interventions (EBIs)

Edmark Reading Program, research-based reading program, 105

Educators
roles/skill sets, 55–58 (*See also* specific roles/skill sets)

Elementary school
comprehensive writing programs for, 133–34

ELLs. *See* English language learners (ELLs)

Encourager, 89

English as a Second Language (ESL), 73

English language learners (ELLs), 70
CSR and, 87
CWPT, reading intervention, 73

ESL. *See* English as a Second Language (ESL)

Evaluation Strategy: Writing, 114, 128
adjustments, 131
effectiveness checks, 130–31
fidelity check, 130
guide for using, 136
implementation steps, 129–30
instructional usage, 129
overview, 129
research-based evidence, 129
usage, outcomes in, 129

Evidence-based assessment, 4

Evidence-based interventions (EBIs), 5, 7, 37, 68. *See also* Evidence-based reading interventions; Evidence-based writing practices
as component of evidence-based practice, 9
as curricular element, 34, 35
fidelity of implementation, 14

Evidence-based mathematics interventions/models
Classwide peer tutoring, 142, 153–54 (*See also* Classwide peer tutoring (CWPT), mathematics intervention)
Cognitive Guided Instruction, 142, 151–53 (*See also* Cognitive Guided Instruction (CGI))
Concrete-Semiconcrete-Abstract sequence, 142, 146–48 (*See also* Concrete-Semiconcrete-Abstract (CSA) sequence)
list of, 142
MATHFACT, 142, 156–58 (*See also* MATHFACT)
Peer-Assisted Learning Strategies, 142, 155–56 (*See also* Peer-Assisted Learning Strategies (PALS), mathematics intervention)
schema-based instruction, 142, 143–46 (*See also* Schema-based instruction (SBI))
Unitary, Decade, Sequence, Separate, Integrated model, 142, 149–51 (*See also* Unitary, Decade, Sequence, Separate, Integrated (UDSSI) model)

Evidence-based practice, 5, 7–10
components of, 7, 8 (*See also* specific components)
implementer of, educators as, 56, 57

Evidence-based reading interventions. *See also* Evidence-based interventions (EBIs)
classwide peer tutoring, 72–74 (*See also* Classwide peer tutoring (CWPT), reading intervention)
Collaborative Strategic Reading, 87–90 (*See also* Collaborative Strategic Reading (CSR))